Praise for
The Microsoft Infused Classroom

A must-read for any educator that wants to blend student-centered innovative pedagogy with the tools that can make it happen. The ideas and passion the authors have for students, teaching, and pedagogy clearly come center stage in this book. *The Microsoft Infused Classroom* will without a doubt help to inspire great change, evolving how we teach and learn.

—**Justin Chando**, principal product manager, Microsoft Education

The Microsoft Infused Classroom is the book for you if you are leading change and working to help your school thrive with modern teaching and learning. Driven by sound pedagogy and digital tools, this book is a must-have for any Microsoft Edu using educator. As you turn the pages, you will find practical and innovative ideas shared by education changemakers to provide your students with quality learning experiences and the power of Office 365!

—**Robyn Hrivnatz**, Microsoft US Education

The Microsoft Infused Classroom promotes inclusion, agency, and creation. If you are looking for edtech tools, tips, and techniques that can make a difference in your classroom, then you are in the right place!

—**Stephen Eustace**, @eustace_stephen, educator and Microsoft Customer Success Manager

If you want to make the most of Microsoft tools in your classroom, you have the right book. Put simply, The Microsoft-Infused Classroom will make you a better educator. Sure, it shows you the tools and apps you can use. But it goes further, incorporating solid pedagogical practices to improve teaching and learning in your classroom. Your Microsoft tools won't be "just another thing" to add to your plate. They'll be your superpower that leads you and your students to bigger and better things!

—**Matt Miller**, keynote speaker, blogger and author of *Ditch That Textbook*

This book is a *must-read* if you are looking to level up the learning in your Microsoft Infused Classroom and beyond! From innovative ideas to practical advice from your fellow educators, this book has it all! As you read, you will learn how to transform learning with technology and shift instructional practices to better support and empower your scholars. Throughout *The Microsoft Infused Classroom*, you will find tips and tools that inspire fun and creativity as well meaningful ways to foster dynamic communication and share authentic student voice. On top of all of that, you will love the visuals, be challenged with critical considerations, and find yourself wanting to bring learning to life in new ways!

—**Ann Kozma**, @annkozma723, Educator Innovation Lead Flipgrid

Microsoft Education has become a leader in educational technology over the past few years, and this book is precisely what is needed to help educators get caught up! *The Microsoft Infused Classroom* is filled with brilliant, ready-to-use ideas and lessons. Reading the book, I particularly loved the way the authors focused on meaningful ways to utilize all of the tools and not just basic tutorials. As a technology coach in a Microsoft Edu district, this book is one of my go-to resources for inspiration on how to help my colleagues, and I recommend it to all!

—**Scott Titmas** @sdtitmas

The authors of *The Microsoft Infused Classroom* provide a powerful combination of big ideas and actionable tips you won't want to miss! I love how they share both an overview of dynamic, tech-friendly tools, and the strategies educators can use to make the most of technology in the classroom. This book is a must-read for anyone curious about how to use the powerful Microsoft tools with a purpose to elevate student voice and choice throughout the school year!

—**Monica Burns**, EdD, author of *Tasks Before Apps* and Founder of ClassTechTips.com

The Microsoft Infused Classroom is a book for every educator and one that will resonate in some way with everyone. A simple glance through the chapters and the topics covered in this book will grab your interest immediately. There are so many great features about this book: encouragement, inspiration, and the right resources to empower educators to make meaningful changes in their teaching practice that will build student confidence in learning and promote student success. Educators will appreciate the book design with the helpful sections such as A Quick Look, Ideas to Try, and Meet the Tools. It will definitely save time for educators, and I appreciate how the book focuses on pedagogy and purpose first! For educators looking to make a difference, I recommend picking up this book and getting started with some of the great ideas and resources shared.

—**Rachelle Dene Poth**, education advisor, Buncee Spanish and STEAM Teacher, Riverview School District, author of *In Other Words, Unconventional Ways to Thrive in EDU*, *The Future is Now*, and *Chart a New Course*

The incredible educators and authors of *The Microsoft Infused Classroom* have written a must-read for all educators! This guidebook puts pedagogy in the forefront and pairs incredible technology tools to redefine the best practices that results in better learning opportunities for all students.

—**Jornea Armant**, @Savvy_Educator, education innovation lead at Flipgrid, Microsoft

As an educator and long-time lover of Microsoft tools in the classroom, this book is a dream come true! It has been an honor to read how pedagogy is and should always be at the forefront, beautifully paired with innovative ways that technology can bring the classroom to life. This book focuses on making thinking visible, giving every student a voice, and allowing students to share their work in a unique way, leveraging incredible tools while keeping students at the center. *The Microsoft Infused Classroom* is the book I wish I'd had when I was first integrating Microsoft tools into my classroom, and I cannot wait to get it into the hands of every educator I know!

—**Jess Boyce**, @jessxbo, education innovation lead at Flipgrid, Microsoft

The Microsoft Infused Classroom is packed full of practical ideas that can be used in any classroom. The book is the perfect recipe for any teacher to make their classroom student centered. As the authors explain, the infusion of technology in our students lives and classroom requires a shift in thinking to make sure tech enhances instruction. Each section is broken down and provides a perfect blend of tool knowledge and effective classroom uses. Tie in the perfect blend of Microsoft tools and I have no doubt you will walk away with ideas that your students will love. Microsoft has made incredible strides in the EDU sector by listening and working directly with educators and the authors have INFUSED these tools in all the right ways.

—**John Bimmerle**, @J_Bimmerle, MIEExpert and edtech enthusiast

HOLLY CLARK & TANYA AVRITH

THE MICROSOFT INFUSED CLASSROOM

A GUIDEBOOK to
MAKING THINKING VISIBLE
and AMPLIFYING STUDENT VOICE

WITH Felisa Ford, Joe & Kristin Merrill, & Natasha Rachell

Foreword by Mike Tholfsen

The Microsoft Infused Classroom
©2020 by Holly Clark and Tanya Avrith

These books are available at special discounts when purchased in quantity for use as premiums, promotions, fundraising and educational use. For inquiries and details, contact the publisher: info@elevatebooksedu.com.

Published by ElevateBooksEdu

Library of Congress Control Number: On File
Paperback ISBN: 978-1-7334814-7-2
eBook ISBN: 978-1-7334814-8-9

Bring meaningful and high energy PD
TO YOUR SCHOOL, DISTRICT OR EVENT.

The Infused Classroom Learning Workshops are designed with an emphasis on purposeful technology integration.

Customized to fit the needs of your school or district, these workshops are among the best, most hands-on PD experiences around.

In these **hands-on and high-energy** workshops, we will look at some of the most popular and simple tools that can be used to amplify teaching and learning in the classroom. While tools are important, understanding the pedagogical ways we can use them to transform teaching is even more critical, and the Infused Classroom Learning Workshops **lay out a path for allowing teachers and students to make meaning of content**. By the end of the day, educators will have learned how to better use technology to support and amplify the learning experiences in their classrooms.

Built around the **learning framework that helps educators make student thinking and learning visible**, these workshops equip teachers with the strategies and tools to hear from every student and give students a way to meaningfully share their work.

Each Infused Classroom Learning Workshop empowers educators to use technology with . . .

- Formative Assessment Ideas
- Differentiated Instruction Techniques
- Demonstrations of Learning
- Tips for Building a Reflective Practice with Technology

To inquire about online courses and speaking engagements, fill out the form: **bit.ly/InfusedPD**

HOW TO USE THE QR CODES
for More Learning Fun!

Throughout the book you will see QR codes every so often. To watch the video attached, simply download the Flipgrid app on your Android or iOS device and open it. Next, select Scan Flipgrid QR. Point at QR code and watch the QR code come to life.

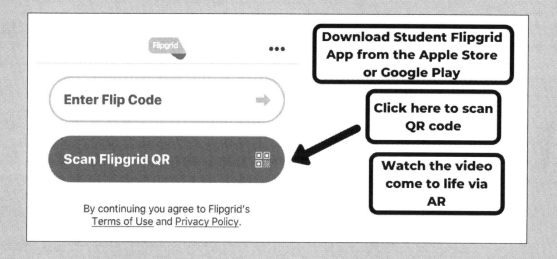

CONTENTS

THE MICROSOFT INFUSED CLASSROOM

is all about putting the student at the center of the classroom, empowering the next generation of great leaders with technology that can adapt and personalize their learning experience to their needs.

FOREWORD
BY MIKE THOLFSEN

When Satya Nadella took the reigns as CEO of Microsoft, one of his first orders was to ensure every employee knew without question what the company stood for, our mission, and reason to exist. Today, ask any employee and they can dutifully recite it for you: "to empower every person and every organization on the planet to achieve more." For me and the hundreds of employees around the world who commit each day to our education technology, that mission starts in the classroom by empowering every educator, administrator, parent, and student with technology that can help them achieve more.

Our mission is both inclusive and expansive, and it aligns directly with the ideas and concepts put forth in *The Microsoft Infused Classroom*. In my role as a product manager, I've had the opportunity to visit and work with some of the most innovative educators and schools in the world, and without a doubt, one of the best parts of my job is when I get to see how educators use our tools in unique and creative ways that we never imagined.

I distinctly remember the first time I met Holly, Joe, and Kristin at Flipgrid Live in Minneapolis in 2018. It was a fitting event for this introduction, surrounded by passionate educators who were changemakers in their communities, much like the group of inspiring educators who've written this book. They are some of the leading thinkers in the education space, and the ideas and passion they have for students, teaching, and pedagogy are helping to motivate great changes, evolving how we teach and learn.

The Microsoft Infused Classroom is all about putting the student at the center of the classroom, empowering the next generation of great leaders with technology that can adapt and personalize their learning experience to their needs. It's about helping today's students see how technology will help them to change the world and giving them the tools and support they need to envision the bold new world they will entering upon graduation. They will take college courses that don't exist yet. They will do jobs that have not yet been created. And they will be asked to tackle some of the most challenging environmental and societal challenges of any generation before them. It's our job to empower them today so they are ready for tomorrow.

This book is a guide with new ideas for effective teaching and learning in the modern classroom, along with useful and practical tips to save teachers valuable time. Most of all, *The Microsoft Infused Classroom* focuses on how to ensure all students can thrive in today's digital classroom environment. It's about making every student feel included with technology that amplifies their potential, something that has become a personal passion of mine as I've traveled the world and have seen the lack of great tools to support diverse learners.

I've had the chance to work, present, brainstorm, and tweet with many of the authors, and I'm continuously inspired by what I see. They are all innovative educators who understand teaching and learning, technology, and most importantly, students. With a new generation of learners coming up, and society's digital transformation only gaining speed, it's vital that educators have a Microsoft Infused Classroom toolkit that can help guide them through the education landscape of both today and tomorrow.

Now you'll have the chance to learn about and bring many of these same practices and scenarios to life in your classroom, with guidance from the authors and free tools you can start using and sharing today!

How to Read This Book

When writing this book, we wanted to address the two common ways to think about transforming learning with technology: pedagogy and tools. We wanted to create an asset that would support and connect both ways of approaching technology integration. Maybe you want to find a better way to assess knowledge and understanding? Start with pedagogy. Or maybe you have heard about screencasting but don't know how to incorporate it into your instruction.

Starting with Pedagogy? Perfect!

The pedagogy section starts here and continues throughout the book. It will give you some context for the learning theories that are the basis of the ideas presented. We'll start with a focus on using technology to make student thinking and learning visible, giving every student a voice, and allowing them to share their work. From there, we'll jump into some basic pedagogical structures and provide some Microsoft Infusions and other online learning tools that will enable you to remain faithful to pedagogy while amplifying your instruction with easy-to-use technology tools.

PEDAGOGY

PEDAGOGY

PED-UH-GOH-JEE

\\'PE-Də-,GŌ-JĒ

NOUN

The method and practice of teaching, especially as an academic subject or theoretical concept.

@HollyClarkEdu

As you sit down to read this book, it is important to understand what is meant by an *Infused Classroom*. It is a three-part concept. First and foremost, it is a student-centered classroom—where students take charge of their learning. Second, the classroom infuses modern tools such as technology to help make student learning more meaningful. Third, it is led by a knowledgeable and evolving teacher.

In an Infused Classroom, the teaching and learning outcomes are the most important aspect, and technology simply enhances an already purposeful learning environment. Here we seek to better understand our students as learners and empower their learning journey. Infused Classrooms, and thus Infused Teachers, combine both great pedagogy and technology, but only when it will make the learning stronger.

With students and learning at the center of an Infused Classroom, teachers can now rethink their own practices and routines. They might spend less time lecturing and more time facilitating as students uncover their own thinking and understanding by piecing ideas together themselves. This classroom seeks to allow students to construct their knowledge, but it never eliminates small doses of necessary direct instruction. Technology assists in making student learning more meaningful and powerful.

An Infused Teacher does not "start over" to infuse technology into their practice. Instead, they think about the lessons they already have that might be enhanced with a new tool or two. Think of an Infused Teacher like a modern chef with a library of great recipes, but maybe after visiting India they decide to add some cumin or turmeric to a traditional sauce. Boom! The flavors come alive. In your classroom, you are simply adding an additional component to make an experience richer, more relevant, and more accessible. You focus on the pedagogy we know works, and then infuse some "flavors" of today, like technology, to make that lesson more profound, more powerful, and more modern. Boom! The learning comes alive.

Let's take a closer look at these three concepts:

THE INFUSED CLASSROOM

The Infused Classroom is about student-centered learning and student thinking. It honors the student, the experience, and the times. We cannot ignore that we are teaching smack dab in the middle of an information revolution, and the Infused Classroom honors this change by giving students new ways to construct and show their learning.

This learning environment takes already great pedagogy such as checks for understanding, differentiation, demonstrations of learning, and reflection, and offers ways technology can enrich those tasks.

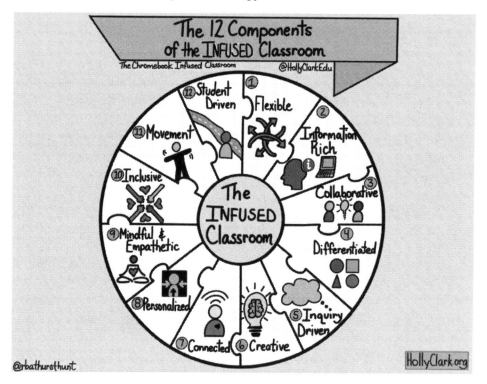

Technology figures prominently, but it comes **second** to great pedagogy focused on learning goals. The classroom is infused with all the strategies and skill acquisition that bring a great learning experience to our students and gives them greater chance for autonomy over their learning.

For more information, see **infused.link/infusedclassroom12**.

INFUSED CLASSROOM TEACHERS
Like the components of The Infused Classroom, no single quality of an Infused Teacher is more important than another; instead, together they provide the whole that is needed to be a teacher in this age of information and monumental change.

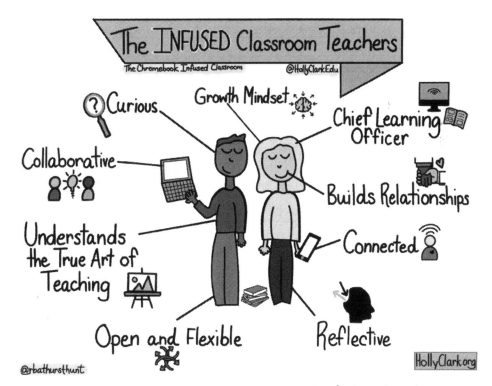

To learn more about this, visit **infused.link/infusedteacher**.

INFUSED CLASSROOM STUDENTS

As educators have access to more and more technology in the classroom, we need to rethink the students' role in learning. In a technology-rich classroom, the role of the student as strictly a memorizer and regurgitator of content MUST change. Students need to see themselves as people in control of their own learning, and not just passive receivers of information.

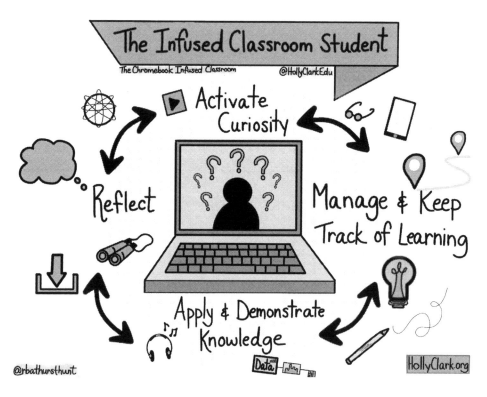

See this blog post for more information: **infused.link/infusedstudent**.

WHY THIS BOOK?

Teachers need ideas for enriching great pedagogy with meaningful technology. In this book, we offer a plan for taking great pedagogical goals and infusing them with the technology to enhance or make them better, more purposeful, and more modern.

In this book, we will be sharing with you how to have a Microsoft Infused Classroom by using the Microsoft tools to make learning more powerful. We have also included a few other tools that you can use within the Microsoft ecosystem to enhance learning and that play well with Microsoft apps.

Ultimately, the Infused Classroom model brings technology and pedagogy together to place students at the center of their own learning. This book is intended to get you started by looking at the pedagogy first and then offers up the tools that will help you reach your intended results in engaging and highly effective ways.

We wish you good luck on your journey to becoming an Infused Teacher! We hope you will share your journey by becoming part of the community.

JOIN THE INFUSED COMMUNITY!

@HollyClarkEdu #infusedclassroom

@TanyaAvrith @apsitnatasha @APSITFelisa @TheMerrillsEdu

Facebook.com/groups/infusedclassroom

EdSpace.Live—Infused Classroom Channel

WHY MICROSOFT

Microsoft is used by students worldwide to infuse their learning using a set of powerful tools that help them become more active in their own learning process. The company is committed to education, and new CEO Satya Nadella is dedicated to ensuring that Microsoft keeps offering tools to make learning more meaningful and accessible. These tools are available for free for teachers and students using Office 365, which is web-based and can be downloaded to your computer and used as a mobile app. This means Microsoft can be used on any device—exciting news!

Recently, Microsoft made a big change to the way people can access the platform. Now, all teachers and students can access their free Microsoft Office 365 accounts by using their Google account logins. This one move will better connect classrooms from around the world and will make it easy for kids from nearly every school to be able to learn together in collaborative and creative ways.

Microsoft has acquired exciting platforms, including teacher-favorite Flipgrid and student-favorite Minecraft, which can be an important creation tool for students to demonstrate their knowledge. The company has made acquisitions like this with the goal of providing truly valuable tools that push forward educational innovation for classrooms.

The Infused Classroom seeks to put the student at the center of their learning and to give students a way to make their thinking and learning visible. In this book, we will examine how we can infuse some of the very powerful Microsoft tools to make student thinking and learning visible and empower education in magical ways.

What is exciting is that teachers everywhere, even those using all different platforms and operating systems, agree that OneNote is one of the finest, most diverse, and easy-to-use tools out there for education. It is a profound instrument in allowing students to easily interact with and keep track of their learning. Now all students, even those with Google accounts, can have access to this instrumental tool.

"Microsoft aims to democratize these tools to empower every educator and student to create the world of tomorrow."

—Satya Nadella, Microsoft CEO

Teachers are excited about how the Microsoft tools allow them to reach all learners. Students can easily collaborate with classes around the globe and quickly make student thinking and learning visible with tools such as Flipgrid.

Microsoft is all about community, and the further you explore all there is to offer teachers, students, and families, the more you realize how great this global family is. The Microsoft learning community is large—regardless of what you are looking to learn, there is someone willing to help. In addition, Microsoft has made accessibility a top priority. *All* students can benefit from tools such as Immersive Reader, which is quickly popping up on all of your favorite apps. Microsoft has realized their impact in this field and has taken many steps to ensure that students everywhere have the same access to these programs. In the words of Marlee Matlin, "No one should have to ask for access—it should just be there."

Putting technology in the hands of students is powerful, but finding ways to meet their unique needs is truly innovating. Microsoft is always listening to educators when it comes to the updates and improvements they release. They value the ideas of educators and work hard to give them tools that will make learning more efficient and accessible for all. Microsoft's goal to make learning accessible for all is something we can get behind!

Disrupting
WHAT IT MEANS TO BE LITERATE

Remember when you had to pay to access WiFi at places like Starbucks? Fortunately, those days are long gone! Businesses have realized that their customers value being connected, so they've made it easy for us to be online while shopping, eating, or waiting to pick up an order.

Our students also desire this connection. Each day, they are sharing pictures and posting status updates online via Snapchat or TikTok—everywhere but in the classroom. Many of them, however, don't know how to share their ideas properly. Nor do they understand how to curate a powerful learning network online, cultivate an idea by finding and connecting with others who share their passions, or develop their ideas into something bigger. They haven't learned how to use the power of the internet and connected learning because schools largely view technology and social media as distractions. Instead of having teachers guide and teach them how to use the incredible tools and information that are available, too many students are left to themselves to learn about being online, often in inappropriate ways.

Why don't schools allow students to connect online? In some cases, lack of funding for technology plays a role. More frequently, though, school bans on social media, internet access, or technology in general is a product of fear, one found in our collective unconscious. Society periodically goes through massive shifts, where both information and how it's distributed changes. During the early stages of each of these shifts, people become uncomfortable. Throughout history, change has always brought about fears of how the new medium will affect society. We can go as far back as the invention of writing, which Socrates warned citizens against, fearing it would "create forgetfulness in the learners' souls, because they will not use their memories." Each technological advancement elicits new fears. With invention of the printing press, people feared that books would make them stupid because they would have no way of knowing the words' and claims' validity. Then the typewriter came along and people asked, "How will kids learn proper penmanship?" With the mobile phone, the worry was that they would cause a distraction in education. Technology and the use of social media

in schools has now created another shift, many people fear (or at least are uncomfortable with) the ways society uses smartphones, mobile technology, and apps to connect and collaborate. These tools put so much of the learning of humankind at our fingertips, and we should consider them as extraordinary rather than dismiss them as distractions. Here's the good news about the naysayers of every shift: They almost always learn to be okay with the invention over time, and some even become proponents of the new technology once they get over their fears.

Redefining Literacy

In some popular science fiction texts, authors present the ideas of a post-literate society in which multimedia technology has advanced to the point where we no longer communicate through reading and writing. With the advent of voice assistants, including Apple's Siri and Amazon's Alexa, it isn't hard to imagine a future that looks just like that. As we move into the twenty-first century, we need to teach our students to be "transliterate"—that is, fluent across all mediums of information, not just reading and writing.

If we're going to prepare our students for a technology-rich future, we must expand the definition of what it means to be literate. We need to create a disruptive shift in how we, as educators, define literacy. An important step toward accurately redefining literacy is to **think of our students as participants in a global society, rather than simply as learners**. After all, in their before-and after-school hours, students already connect in unprecedented ways. As connected global participants, they will need to develop crucial skills, including networked learning (an important part of the redefinition process) and the ability to understand and use different and new media. Before we can teach them how to develop and use these twenty-first-century skills, we must understand the process ourselves so that we can serve as our students' Sherpas and help them explore these new forms of literacy.

Jump In

Most of us surf the internet and post to Facebook, but those activities are not enough to understand the real power of learning one can experience online. If Facebook is your connection of choice, it is important to understand a few important facts: Facebook leans toward being more about social sharing than social learning, and the average Facebook user is 41.5 years old. What's more, although students are still using Facebook, they prefer Instagram, Snapchat, TikTok, and YouTube.

With social media replacing newspapers and television as one of the first sources where people learn about the day's news and products, students need to be savvy about online information—how to find it, validate it, and then make sense of it. And if our students are to be successful in their future careers, they'll need to understand social media marketing, including tweets, retweets, hashtags, followers, and how to improve search engine optimization (SEO) rankings.

As disruptive, transliterate educators, we must learn how to speak social media and understand what it means to be connected learners so that we can guide our students. We must know and understand these new forms of information—how to use them correctly, what their nuances are, and how they are shaping our world. We must know how to curate information and crowdsource comprehension. In the end, we must

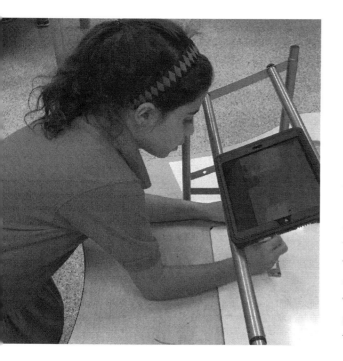

teach our students transliteracy and shift their focus from simply reading and writing to developing and using all of the communication skills they'll need to achieve success in our modern society.

Think of what it takes to become a chef: If all chefs-in-training did was read cookbooks, take tests about what they read, and write about ingredients, chances are they probably wouldn't cook very well. The art of cooking requires understanding flavors, knowing which tools to use for which purposes, and being familiar with the different ways to develop a dish. Until would-be chefs actually experiment with recipes, it is difficult for them to truly know how to cook. They must prove their ability to cook before they are called chefs. So how could they possibly learn how to become chefs if they have a teacher who believes in experimenting with spices and herbs is a distraction?

The same principle applies to learning. Instead of simply reading the cookbook, start cooking—or, in our case, join Twitter. And if Twitter isn't for you, follow some blogs or create an Instagram account so you can better understand where your students are and how you can turn these social media platforms into a powerful learning tools within your classroom.

Being a disruptive teacher means understanding that although students know how to use technology, they don't understand how to use it to learn. It means speaking social media and understanding connected learning—and realizing the profound impact of both.

As teachers, we need to curate a network of educators who are doing great things in their classrooms, a network of colleagues who will introduce us to ideas and innovations, and people whom we can reach out to with questions. We should follow experts and learners alike who share creative ideas for helping our students become life-ready.

Connecting will serve as your roadmap, and your colleagues will become your guides—your own personal Sherpas—to creating a more innovative, disruptive classroom, where learning once again becomes a more relevant endeavor and literacy is transformed. Only once we know better can we do better.

> "I did then what I knew how to do. Now that I know better, I do better."
>
> **—Maya Angelou**

Ten Characteristics
OF OUR GENERATION Z LEARNERS

1

They are the first real digital natives. They have never known a world without smartphones, tablets, and social media.

They expect technology; they need dynamic, interactive content; and they want to create more than just PowerPoint presentations.

2

They talk in images (e.g., emojis, pictures, and videos).

Find ways to use Adobe Spark, Flipgrid, and photo apps in your classroom and allow students to explain their understanding using pictures, graphs, and **infographics**.

3

They are social entrepreneurs and like their learning to have meaning and purpose.

You can nurture their passions by allowing them to do Genius Hour or **20% Time** projects or even create a real business.

** Bold/underlined words are defined in "Ideas to Try" on page 40.

We generally define "Generation Z" as people born between 1995 and 2010. However, some thought leaders claim Gen Z is less of a generation and more of a mindset that we can all adopt—if we aspire to learn, unlearn, and relearn.

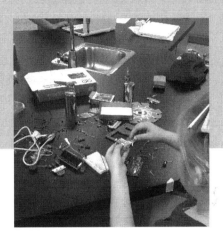

They think in 4-D and 360-degree, and high-definition videos.

Bringing VR into your classroom is a great idea! Better yet, buy a Ricoh Theta and have students create their own 360-degree video content.

They prefer to do hands-on and interactive projects.

Consider having students do projects that are in line with their learning style, like something musical or kinesthetic, or have them learn to code using apps like Scratch or Minecraft Education Edition.

Ten Characteristics
OF OUR GENERATION Z LEARNERS

6

They communicate in short, bite-sized ideas.

Allow students to tweet with authors, teach them how to write effective comments and reviews. Try the a six-word summary project using Adobe Spark Post.

7

They like to create.

You can empower students to think creatively by learning to code, creating a book with Book Creator or working through a problem with SolveinTime.com.

8

Their social circle is global.

Allow students to connect with experts and peers who are from other geographical areas who have different perspectives. This allows them to crowdsource multiple views in their learning, which can harness the power of empathy and compassion.

9

Their cell phones are the hub of their social lives, with their apps of choice being Snapchat, Instagram, and Tik Tok.

Consider ways to safely introduce these apps into your classroom. Try **BookSnaps** or SnapStories.

10

They want to win using strategies, practice, and do-overs.

You can help them win by teaching learning strategies such as **sketchnoting** and by gamifying your classroom.

A Quick Look
AT LEARNING THEORIES

Constructivism and Connectivism

Clearly, your Generation Z students are primed for learning that integrates technology. As you design your lessons, consider how drawing upon the constructivism and connectivism learning theories could help you effectively deliver instruction in a way that meets your twenty-first-century learners' needs and expectations while also helping prepare them for their future. Here's a quick recap of these two theories and how they might help you improve the learning experiences in your classrooms.

Constructivism is based on the idea that students construct knowledge and meaning through experiences. Students need to work with information, play with it, try new ways, figure things out on their own (and in their own way), find other views and opinions, and come to their own understanding of concepts. In addition, they need to construct their own understanding and knowledge by reflecting on those experiences. Constructivism is based in Jean Piaget's theory of cognitive development which states that humans cannot be fed or given information for learning. Instead, we must construct knowledge.

A Constructivist Classroom

- Places students at the center
- Is activity-based
- Is noisy and full of movement
- Encourages students to become expert learners
- Includes problem-based learning
- Applies real-world problems to concepts
- Allows time for reflection
- Values meaning over facts
- Offers differentiated activities that build upon students' strengths and weaknesses
- Wants students to construct knowledge and create demonstrations of learning, not memorize and recite facts
- Has students taking on a major role in determining the direction of their learning and what that learning process looks like

Connectivism proposes that students learn through their connections and networks, both physical and digital. Developed by Canadian researchers Stephen Downes, the originator of the MOOC (Massive Open Online Course) and George Siemens, author of the book *Knowing Knowledge*, connectivism theory suggests that learning happens when students consult a diversity of opinions, use networks to find and validate relevant, up-to-date information, and utilize a crowd as the source of information. As educators, we must teach our students how to learn in a world where their social network can become a direct or even unintended teacher. Likewise, we must teach them how to critically think their way through the process and understand these new modes of learning.

A Connectivist Classroom

- Encourages students to blog with people from around the world

- Acknowledges the power of Twitter to grow a community of people passionate about a subject

- Allows students to publish their work in portfolios and gather feedback

- Encourages students to write collaboratively with peers from other countries

- Makes Mystery Skypes, during which students guess their Skype partner's location, commonplace

- Teaches students how to effectively find and validate information online

- Elicits a variety of opinions through Twitter, Instagram, and blogs

- Understands how to find new, important learning channels

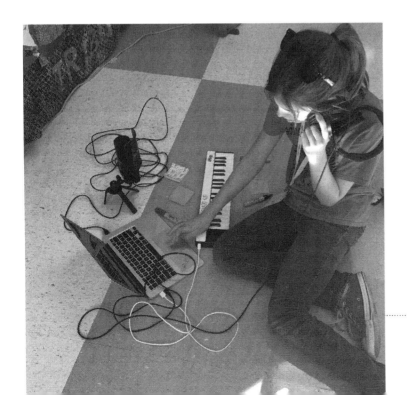

Making Thinking Visible
GIVING EVERY STUDENT A VOICE AND SHARING STUDENTS' WORK

Throughout this book, you'll find three core ideas that we believe are essential to education: making thinking visible, giving every student a voice, and allowing students to share their work. Having worked in technology-infused classrooms for the past two decades, we've concluded that effective technology integration happens when educators ask themselves these questions:

- How can I make student thinking visible?

- How can I use the technology to hear from every student in the class?

- How can I allow students to actively share their work so that they can learn from one another?

When students are allowed to use technology to write papers or take notes, it certainly making their lives easier, but replacing pen and paper with technology doesn't equate to making real advances in the way we use technology in schools. Our goal (we hope yours, as well) is to ensure that we're using technology in ways that will help students **make bigger gains in their academic growth** and also **allow us to understand where they are in their learning process** so we can quickly make changes in our instructional coaching and help them succeed. That means their thinking and learning must be visible.

Making Thinking (and Learning) Visible

In the past, it was difficult to help our students visualize their thinking because we didn't have time to hear from each and every student and listen to their reflections very often. But thanks to today's technology, getting inside our students' heads and finding out what they know and don't know is easier than ever. We can ask students to reveal their insights by offering the use of apps that allow them to articulate and record their learning experiences, ideas, and thinking. This is especially important because at the foundation of all good, cognitive learning

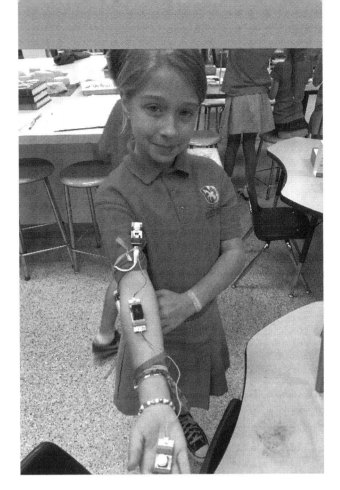

is the idea that we must teach our students how to think about thinking (metacognition). Fortunately, our Gen Z students are characterized by their ability to learn, unlearn, and relearn ideas and concepts. Because our information landscape is rapidly changing, this ability is growing in importance and becoming even more essential to teach.

To understand how students learn best, though, we must first learn how to make their thinking visible by using "thinking routines," or methods for questioning the learning process. In their book, *Making Thinking Visible*, authors Ron Ritchhart, Mark Church, and Karin Morrison describe these thinking routines, many of which classrooms use to uncover the root of the thinking process. Take, for example, this key thinking routine from their book, which shows us how students' thinking has changed: "I used to think … but now I think … " The key here is making these processes part of the very fabric of our classrooms so that students intuitively activate them to make connections and deepen their reflections. This book will show you how to easily integrate technology tools in ways that will allow for deeper reflective learning and help students better understand their own thinking and learning processes.

Thinking routines remind us that learning is not a product, but a process of understanding. During that process, we should encourage our students to verbalize and explain what they're learning, as well as what is and isn't working, what struggles they're facing, what comes easily, and whether they believe they've reached the learning target. At that point, they should offer demonstrations of their learning to show they've reached the goal. We also call these demonstrations of learning "assessments for learning," and students should do them throughout their learning process so they can gain insights into how they learn best.

In all likelihood, your classroom is filled with technology. The ideas and tools discussed in this book will help you use that technology to quickly and efficiently unveil your students' thinking and understanding.

Student Voice

Think back to when you were a student. There were probably about four or five of your peers who always raised their hands first to answer any question. As a result, your teacher heard from these eager students frequently but had limited information about where the rest of the students in the class were in the learning process.

Beyond having the obvious problem of getting everyone's active participation, the tools traditionally used to gather information about students' learning, like fill-in-the-blank and multiple-choice questions, don't give us a good opportunity to really understand our students as individuals, but, rather, as kids who complete tasks. Based on these answers, we learn very little about how students come to their conclusions or about what they really understand.

Thanks to technology, though, we can now ask a question of and hear from every child in the room, even the ones who are too shy or too scared to answer out loud. We can do this in about two minutes, which is less time than it would take to gather answers from those with their hands up and even less time than it takes to write down an answer.

Check out this site for a quick-start guide and resource on thinking routines:

infused.link/thinkingroutines

For example, when we were kids, our teachers would have us respond to questions by writing the answers on a piece of paper, then tell us to place the paper with the answers upside-down, pass them forward, and sit quietly as they were collected. It was as if we were sharing top-secret information only our teacher could read. Days would pass before we received feedback, and by the time the teacher knew if we understood the lesson, class was long over. Sadly, even the interval she spent collecting the papers resulted in lost learning time. Thankfully, today's technology and tools have changed all that.

If you aren't hearing from every student in your class during crucial learning segments, it may be because you're not using technology to its full abilities. The great news is you can! For example, using an app like Socrative, you can ask a "Quick Question" from the Launchpad. Students enter your virtual room and quickly respond to the prompt. As the responses populate on the screen, you can easily ascertain what the students have learned and where some understanding may still be lacking. With this information, you can adjust your lesson in real time—based on the individual needs of your students.

Sharing Student Work

When we use technology to upgrade our learning, it can have profound effects on students. Take sharing student work, for example: By incorporating visual thinking apps like Padlet, Socrative, and Seesaw into this process, students can watch their peers' responses come in, compare their answers, make adjustments to incorrect thinking, and maybe even learn something from the posted answers. It's during this sharing process that students are plunged into a state of metacognition—when they are thinking about their thinking.

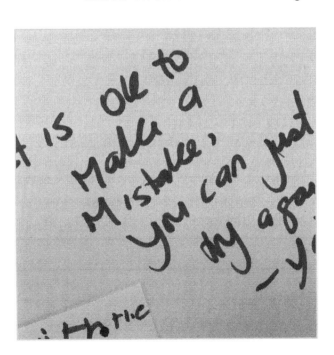

We realize traditional teaching methods often frown upon students seeing one another's answers, but this is a learning fallacy, and it's one that needs to change. Keeping student work private ignores the foundational theory of constructivism, which states that people construct knowledge and meaning from their experiences. In short, students learn best from one another, and seeing another student's answers can often result in important "light bulb" moments.

Additionally, students want to put their best foot forward when they know their work will be seen by someone other than their teacher. You'll notice that when your students know their work will be shared with the class, the school, or even with the world online, they will begin taking the time to construct very critical, well-thought-out responses.

Employing these three techniques—making thinking visible, using technology to hear from every student, and allowing students to share their work—affects student growth in a way that empowers them to understand how they learn. In effect, they learn about learning. When we combine these techniques with having students create demonstrations of learning to reflect on their learning process, such as explaining how they met the target, that's when the magic really happens. It's then that technology becomes something more than a word processor or powerful internet searcher—it amplifies the learning process.

Consider This …
HOW TECHNOLOGY CAN IMPROVE LEARNING

Before you integrate technology into your classroom, ask yourself these questions:

1 Is my goal to teach the technology or the content?

2 Is this form of technology how my student learns best? Does it support their learning abilities?

3 Are all of my students doing the same project? If they are, is that the best way for each individual learner to demonstrate their understanding of the learning targets?

4 Am I using the technology to amplify skills like collaboration, consumption, or critical thinking? Does the tool encourage students to be curious or create?

5 How does using the technology give me rich information about the student's learning and growth? What new and insightful information can I gather about the learner from the project?

6 Am I integrating technology for the sake of integrating technology, or to make my lessons better, more powerful, more collaborative, and easier to access from outside the classroom?

7 Will the technology empower my students to do things I'd never imagined, things that go beyond my classroom's four walls when I was a student?

8 Have my students received any instruction on how to use the tool? Do they know what good design looks like? Have I talked to them about fonts? Do they know how to make insightful and meaningful comments?

9 Do my students know how to effectively search for and validate information online?

10 How are the social media and blog posts I'm asking my students to write driving learning and curiosity in my class?

"A lot of scientific evidence suggests that the difference between those who succeed and those who don't is not the brains they were born with, but their approach to life, the messages they receive about their potential, and the opportunities they have to learn."

—Jo Boaler, *Mathematical Mindsets: Unleashing Students' Potential through Creative Math, Inspiring Messages and Innovative Teaching*

A Quick Look
AT UbD

Understanding by Design (UbD) is based on the belief that teachers should design instruction backwards. It is a three-step process that **identifies the desired results, determines the acceptable evidence, and plans the learning experiences and instruction accordingly.** The framework gives teachers the flexibility to allow each student to progress toward this learning target in different ways. You might start with an essential question that students work toward answering, whether that's a student-generated question or one you've crafted for the unit.

According to ASCD UbD White Paper from March 2012, "Backward design encourages teachers and curriculum planners to first think like assessors before designing specific units and lessons. The assessment evidence we need reflects the desired results identified."

Students need to be able to show their understanding and progression toward the learning goal, and according to the UbD framework, they do this through the lens of the six facets of understanding:

1. They can **explain** the learning goal.

2. They **interpret** it.

3. They **apply** it.

4. They can **understand different perspectives**.

5. They **show empathy**.

6. They **demonstrate a metacognitive awareness** of the material and their learning.

McTighe and Wiggins explain that the main goal of the student is "transfer of learning" and making meaning of the experience.

This framework will be the basis of the next four sections, how we approach the desired results we are looking for, and the way we view learning.

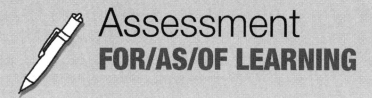

Assessment
FOR/AS/OF LEARNING

Before we begin our roadmap to effective technology integration, here is a breakdown of Assessment For/As/Of Learning.

Assessment for Learning

An **assessment for learning**, or formative assessment, is exactly what it sounds like: It's an assessment that helps us understand where our students are in the learning process. However, in this case, we don't grade these assessments. Rather, when done properly, they provide us and each of our students with ongoing, real-time feedback about where they are in their learning and what interventions they may need to achieve success. These assessments also allow us to make just-in-time adjustments to our classroom instruction and provide students with valuable insights into which areas they may need to focus their attention.

Assessment as Learning

An **assessment as learning** is an ongoing assessment that students do to reflect on and monitor their progress. By asking students to record their reflections and processes using a tool like OneNote, we're encouraging them to think about their learning process, make their thinking visible, and help them take responsibility for achieving their personal learning goals. By doing this type of assessment, students are more likely to ask for and receive feedback from others. This feedback can be critical to helping them understand their own areas of strength and need.

Assessment of Learning

An **assessment of learning** is the "summative evaluation" of a student's work. In this case, we measure a student's work against the predetermined learning criteria to see if they've demonstrated an understanding of the intended learning targets. Generally, students' final creations and work give us more insight into their learning and personal growth than an assessment based in multiple-choice questions ever could.

Consideration: Typically, summative assessments that take place at the end of a unit and look at a standardized proficiency, judging individual students by everyone else's progress. Instead of asking the same questions and having a blanket target for all of our students, though, we should look for student growth on an individual scale. We should find out what each student knows at the beginning of a unit then determine individualized targets. This allows us to throw out percentages and measure our well-defined learning targets against the student-led conferences and evidence of learning we glean from their portfolios, thereby letting us grade each student on their individual growth, not where we expect everyone to be.

Flipgrid
flipgrid.com

Flipgrid is a video response platform that allows students to view posted topics, record their responses, and reply to their classmates. It can be found online at flipgrid.com, inside the Office portal at office.com, or inside of Microsoft Teams.

MEET THE TOOLS

Teams
teams.office.com

Microsoft Teams is a collaboration software that is part of the Office 365 suite of applications. Microsoft Teams allows messaging, calling, video meetings, and file sharing. Microsoft Teams serves as a digital hub for teachers to house all content, conversations, and apps in one place, including assigning and grading assignments.

OneNote
onenote.office.com

OneNote is a digital notebook that is part of the Office 365 suite of apps that allows you to create digital notebooks. It also allows for digital inking. OneNote promotes ease of use and organization by allowing users to organize their notebooks into sections and pages, as well as providing the ability to search the notebook for specific content. Users are able to type, highlight, and annotate notes and retrieve them across all devices. With OneNote, users are able to easily share and collaborate with their peers.

Sway
sway.office.com

Sway is a cloud-based Office 365 tool that allows students and teachers to create individual or collaborative reports, presentations, newsletters, and more. With built-in artificial intelligence (AI) features, Sway provides effortless design ideas, which allows users to focus on the content.

Immersive Reader

Immersive Reader takes accessibility to the next level by creating a full-screen reading experience to increase readability of content. It was designed to help students with dyslexia and dysgraphia, but it also can support primary students or struggling readers.

Microsoft Forms
forms.office.com

Microsoft Forms is an Office 365 app and online platform that is easy to use and lets users create a variety of response formats such as surveys, quizzes, polls, and feedback, to name a few. MS Forms allows for the real-time collection of responses, which results in data being quickly visualized and analyzed based on the responses. MS Forms is integrated with many of the Office 365 apps to promote ease of use.

Book Creator
app.bookcreator.com

Book Creator is a website that can be accessed from Edge that allows students to create books, comics, journals, and authentic learning artifacts. They can publish and share their creations online for others to view and read.

Adobe Spark
spark.adobe.com

Adobe Spark is the integrated web and mobile solution that enables everyone, especially teachers and their students of all ages, to easily create and share impactful visual stories. Adobe Spark supports three story formats and three ways to express ideas:

- Adobe Spark Video lets you turn your story into a captivating animated narrated video in just minutes.

- Adobe Spark Page turns stories into modern, professional, attention-grabbing web pages.

- Adobe Spark Post enables you to create stunning graphics in seconds.

Pear Deck
peardeck.com

Pear Deck allows teachers to create interactive presentations that can be accessed by students in real time.

Teachers create experiences that can be pushed out to all students simultaneously or create self-paced experiences.

MEET THE TOOLS

Buncee
app.edu.buncee.com

Buncee is a creation and communication tool for both students and teachers that empowers users to create and share content. It meets the criteria for an effective tool by being powerful, easy to use, and manageable—applicable across grade levels and subject areas.

Seesaw
web.seesaw.me

Seesaw is a comprehensive easy-to-use digital portfolio app and website that gives students a platform to collaborate and share their learning.

Socrative
socrative.com

Socrative is a website app that allows you to quickly gather information about your students' learning in the form of closed and open-ended questions.

Microsoft Learning Tools

infused.link/learningtools

Microsoft Learning Tools are designed to support students with dyslexia and dysgraphia in the classroom but can support anyone who wants to make reading on their device easier, communicate with others, or get math support.

PowerPoint

powerpoint.office.com

PowerPoint is the all-inclusive presentation creator. Features such as AI designer, captioning, and translation and presenter coach all help students demonstrate their learning by building presentations.

Minecraft: Education Edition

education.minecraft.net

Minecraft: Education Edition is the education version of the popular infinite world game-based platform that promotes creativity, collaboration, and critical thinking while also being aligned to K-12 content standards. Minecraft: Education Edition includes classroom features that promote and support formative assessment, coding, project-based learning, twenty-first-century skills, and design thinking and innovation.

Wakelet

wakelet.com

Wakelet is a free platform that allows you to curate and organize content to save and share. You can save videos, articles, images, tweets, links, or even add your own text. Save this content in your bookmarks, or organize related items into a collection.

Microsoft Educator Community

infused.link/mseducation

The Microsoft Educator Community (MEC) is a free web-based platform that is specifically dedicated to supporting and training educators in the use of Microsoft tools and resources for teaching and learning. Teachers have access to online courses, they can earn badges, and they can collaborate with educators from around the world.

WHAT THE TOOLS DO

COLLABORATE

Microsoft Word
PowerPoint
Flipgrid
Padlet
Seesaw
OneNote
Teams

CREATE VIDEOS

Flipgrid
Screencast-O-Matic
Adobe Spark Video
PowerPoint

PUBLISH

Flipgrid
Seesaw
Sway
Adobe Spark Page and Video

SCREENCAST

Screencast-O-Matic
Seesaw
Flipgrid
PowerPoint

IMAGE EDITING

Adobe Spark Post
Buncee
PowerPoint
Seesaw

CREATE BOOKS/JOURNALS

Adobe Spark Page
OneNote
Word
Seesaw

PowerPoint
Sway
Buncee
Book Creator

DIGITAL PORTFOLIOS

Sway
Seesaw
Adobe Spark Page
OneNote

CREATE PRESENTATIONS

PowerPoint
Buncee
Flipgrid
Sway

CREATE AUDIO FILES

Seesaw
PowerPoint
OneNote
Flipgrid

SHOW WHAT YOU KNOW/ FORMATIVE ASSESSMENT

Seesaw
Socrative
Adobe Spark Page
Adobe Spark Video

Flipgrid
OneNote
Sway
Book Creator

Which tool
SHOULD YOU USE?

Here are some examples to help you make the best decisions. Teachers are always looking for ways to use technology to upgrade what's already working in the classroom. This chart will help you decide which tools will best help you integrate technology in your classroom.

Use these tips as a starting point, and as you create your own INFUSIONS, be sure to share your ideas on Twitter or Instagram, using the hashtag #infusedclassroom.

WERE YOU DOING THIS...	TRY THIS!
Have students make presentations	Edit a video, screencast slides to explain learning. Tell a story using Minecraft: Education Edition.
Complete worksheets, even digital ones	Use an avatar or meme to retell the story. Use Seesaw or Flipgrid to explain a concept. Make video tutorials and share on Padlet or Flipgrid. Allow students to sketchnote their learning in OneNote. Create videos showing what words mean. or develop synonym journals (learn vocabulary). Create digital breakouts using OneNote.
Build dioramas	Create a virtual world in cospaces.io/edu or Minecraft: Education Edition.

Complete homework packets	Create a family cookbook in Adobe Spark Page, play outside with friends, read interest-driven books, have discussions with family members, or start a family-run side business. Use Flipgrid to share learning and experiences. Allow students to sketchnote their learning in OneNote.
Read textbooks	Create content-related HyperDocs, make and upload content-specific videos in Adobe Spark, or create books through Book Creator for next year's class. Create collections in Wakelet of reading and resources around a content or idea.
Take multiple-choice tests and fill out worksheets	Choose the Short Answer Quick Question option in Socrative, show your learning in Seesaw, and discuss the learning process and what you learned in Flipgrid or by using the audio feature within OneNote.
Do workbooks	Make interactive notebooks in OneNote. This way, students create their own learning examples and have them in a notebook or blog to refer to when needed.
Take spelling tests	Create a word studies journal, where, instead of memorizing unrelated words, you study word spelling patterns, roots, prefixes, and other parts, using OneNote. Have students use the drawing/writing feature within OneNote to write their spelling words and then incorporate the audio recording feature to spell and speak their spelling words. Use Flipgrid for students to verbally take their spelling tests.
Fill in reading logs	Share BookSnaps on Padlet or Wakelet Make a Book Channel (Grid) in Flipgrid. Create a Buncee to summarize a book chapter or entire novel.
Partake in round-robin reading	Create reading fluency journals in Seesaw or OneNote. Create a Flipgrid read-aloud grid and go through a story page by page or chapter by chapter.
Design brochures	Create Adobe pages or infographics on Adobe Spark Post. Use Sway to create an interactive infographic.

Create posters	Create a graphic digitally, using Adobe Spark Post or Page—but make sure to explain your thinking by using Seesaw or Flipgrid when you are finished.
	Create a graphic in Buncee and share in Flipgrid or Seesaw—making sure to explain the thinking on both apps.
Participate in linear notetaking	Sketchnote and participate in collaborative notetaking using OneNote.
Take standardized tests	Create powerful narrated demonstrations of learning and curate digital portfolios.
Write book reports	Create "book trailers," using Adobe Spark Video.
	Record videos in Seesaw that describe, review, and rate a book.
	Create a collaborative Amazon-style review grid using Flipgrid. You can then link those reviews to a QR code that you print and attach to hard-copy versions of a book for people to scan and watch your reviews.
	Write and record a movie pitch for the book to present to a Hollywood producer, using Adobe Spark Video, Seesaw, or Flipgrid.
	Collect items in a book box that represent key objects in the story, then either write or create a book Bento Box. Make the image in Adobe Spark Post, Buncee, or PowerPoint, and share out using Padlet.
	For more on Book Bento's see **infused.link/bookbento**.

Pedagogy +
TOOLS TO USE

Well-planned instructional design is the foundation of good teaching. As we've discussed, the better insight you have into your students' understanding, the better able you will be to design a learning experience that meets their needs. In the next sections, we are going to look at how we can use technology tools to make student thinking visible. The journey begins with formative assessment using tools that target student thinking and allow you to hear from every student in the class. Next, based on data you collect from the formative assessment pieces, you will most likely discover that students are progressing in different ways and that you need to offer them different and targeted resources to help them make the most of their learning strengths. This step includes giving students an individualized means of showing growth with demonstrations of learning. Finally, we will explore the importance of reflection.

All of these processes will be based in the Understanding by Design framework for teaching by Jay McTighe and Grant Wiggins. This framework is meant to help teachers (1) identify the learning goals, (2) determine what evidence will prove students have met their goals, and (3) begin planning instruction. This is called "beginning with the end in mind," and is a researched-based approach on how students can show us their learning and understanding.

Ideas to Try
IN *YOUR* CLASSROOM

As you progress through the book, you may find you are not familiar with a few terms. In an effort to make the information more clear, we have provided this glossary of ideas to try that will serve as a reference and a place to find more information on the ideas presented.

100 Word Challenge

This is a weekly creative writing challenge based on a prompt, which can be a picture or a series of words. In just one hundred words, students must write a creative response and then share it on the 100 Word Challenge website (100WC.net). They can then share, view, and comment on examples from around the globe.

Visit **100WC.net** for more information.

BookSnaps

BookSnaps are the perfect way to engage your students in the reading process. Using the very popular social networking app Snapchat, students read, pick a passage to engage with (connect with the content), snap a picture of the passage, doodle on it to show meaning (show their thinking), then share it with their peers. Students could also take a photo of their favorite quote and high-light it, using words or a Bitmoji or even create a meme. You can use Seesaw as an alternative for younger students.

Check out #BookSnaps as well as founder Tara Martin's Twitter page (@TaraMartinEDU) for creative ideas.

Design Thinking

Design thinking is a human- or student-centered process based on empathy that is used to help solve problems and find solutions. Many students and schools use the design thinking model set forth by Stanford's d.school. We recommend **solveintime.com** for a great resource on this and an easy way to get started with problem solving with students.

Here is a Wakelet collection on it: **infused.link/solve**

Differentiate

Differentiating instruction is based on the idea that you need to determine where your students are in their learning process through formative assessments, then design your lessons and resources to meet their learning styles and growth trajectory. *The Differentiated School* author Carol Tomlinson, EdD, calls this "active planning for and attention to student differences in classrooms."

Freemium

This describes a software or web service that provides some of its services for free but charges to access its premium features.

HyperDocs

HyperDocs are based in Google Docs but can do just as well in OneNote and Sway. HyperDocs start with curated links that move students through a lesson design. It allows you to package lesson plans with your students in mind; create learning experiences that emphasize how students learn, rather than simply what they learn; and take advantage of the many web resources available. (For more information about HyperDocs, see this section under "Differentiation." Also check out *The HyperDoc Handbook,* written by Lisa Highfill, Kelly Hilton, and Sarah Landis, on Amazon.

Infographics

Infographics are images representing data or information in an easy-to-read, visually appealing way. Use Adobe Spark Post for this.

Learning Journals

A learning journal lets students keep track of their learning over time, allowing them and you to get a longitudinal view of their progress.

Metacognition

Literally translated from Greek, *metacognition* means "beyond meaning." It is the process of going beyond learning and moving toward gaining an awareness and understanding of our thought processes or, more simply put, thinking about thinking.

Multiple Intelligences

Harvard University professor Howard Gardner, PhD, proposes that, instead of a single IQ, humans possess many types of intelligence, each representing a different way of processing information. These intelligences include verbal-linguistic, logical-mathematical, visual-spatial, musical, naturalistic, bodily-kinesthetic, interpersonal, and intrapersonal.

Mystery Skype

A Mystery Skype brings two classes together, with each class developing a series of educated questions to help them intelligently deduce the location of the other class or school. In this scenario, kids get to apply and use geographical knowledge, critical thinking, and the skill of deduction to figure out where the other students are located. Most teachers structure this activity around the twenty questions model and have students ask each other one question at a time about their geographical location.

Philosophical Chairs

Similar to a debate, Philosophical Chairs is a kinesthetic activity built around constructing knowledge. Start by giving your students a central topic or question that they must choose to agree or disagree with or remain neutral about. Students then either stand or sit in areas designated as "agree," "disagree," or "neutral." One at a time, students speak, trying to convince their peers that their side is the right one. As their peers hear the statements, they can change their position and move to the other areas. This exciting activity typically lasts about twenty minutes and ends with a reflection or debrief of some sort.

Reading Fluency Journals

Students capture their reading fluency by recording themselves reading a story that has been placed on the screen of an app—in this case, we recommend Seesaw or Flipgrid. Students progress through the story on the screen as the app records their voice reading the excerpt. They do this several times during the year to capture a longitudinal journal of their reading abilities and growth.

Screencasts

A screencast (or screen capture) is a digital recording of a screen and often lets you narrate what you're seeing and thinking.

Six-Word Summaries

This technique requires students to think critically about which six words best summarize an activity, idea, or information—think of it as profound brevity. Sample task: Summarize your favorite book in six words.

Sketchnoting

Sketchnoting is a strategy in which students draw pictures and write words in a way that connects to the information or captures a theme, using an app such as OneNote. For more on sketchnoting, visit this Wakelet collection: **infused.link/sketchnoting**.

Student Agency

This is a form of deeper learning that requires students to think, question, pursue, and create to take ownership of their learning.

Video Reflective Journals

These are chronological, diary-like collections of student learning. They house students' video reflections of their thinking, reading fluency, and even language or content acquisition. Over time, students refer back to these journals. We recommend making these reflective recordings using screencasting, Flipgrid, or Seesaw.

Word Studies

Word Studies serve as an alternative to the traditional spelling instructions, in that they're based on students learning word patterns, rather than memorizing unconnected words. Go to **ReadingRockets.org** for more information.

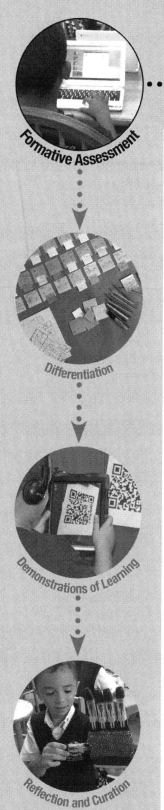

Formative Assessment

Differentiation

Demonstrations of Learning

Reflection and Curation

Tips for
FORMATIVE ASSESSMENT

WHY WE DO THIS: As discussed earlier, an assessment for learning, or formative assessment, is exactly what it sounds like: It's an assessment that helps teachers understand where their students are in the learning process. Following the principles of Understanding by Design (UbD), formative assessment is where we look for acceptable evidence of moving toward the learning goal. These assessments are not meant for grading. They are meant to give us some indicator of where the students are in the learning process. We don't grade formative assessments, because students deserve the opportunity to fully develop, make mistakes, and learn before they are graded on the material. When done properly, these assessments provide us and our students with ongoing, real-time feedback about where they are in their learning and what interventions they may need to achieve success.

These assessments also allow us to make just-in-time adjustments to our classroom instruction and provide students with valuable insights into which areas they may need to focus their attention. The sooner the student understands how they did on these assessments, the better. That is why we seek to make student thinking visible in this process—not only to the teacher but also to the students themselves. Formative assessments provide opportunities for students to engage in metacognitive reflection on their learning; it's during these activities that they can start thinking about their thinking and making their own adjustments as well. If done correctly, each formative assessment should lead the students down a path on which their understanding and performance grow closer and closer to the learning target.

Strategy

Here is where we make student thinking visible. Formative assessment is crucial to understanding what they know, what they have learned, or where they might still need further help.

FIRST, it's time to check in and see where your students are in their learning process. These are informal checks and not meant to be graded.

NEXT, depending on the learning target, you might choose one of the tools in this section to help make your students thinking visible. Each tool will provide a different avenue for achieving this. For example, Socrative is best for text-based answers, Seesaw and OneNote are great for having students provide graphical representations of learning, and Flipgrid is for more audio-based information. Each of the tools provides a wide range of opportunities to gather rich information about student learning and growth.

FINALLY, based on the types of data these tools provide, you might find that you need to change your instruction or begin the process of differentiation.

TOOLS:

Microsoft Forms

Pear Deck

Seesaw

OneNote

Flipgrid

Socrative

MICROSOFT FORMS

ACCESS FROM ANY DEVICE: forms.office.com
FOR MORE IDEAS, HEAD TO infused.link/assessmentforms

WHAT IS MICROSOFT FORMS? Microsoft Forms is the simple Office 365 assessment and survey tool that lets you capture real-time student responses and visualize the response data in charts or spreadsheets, creating a quick and easy way to view student data. Microsoft Forms is available online or as a stand-alone application.

This platform lets you create various forms for quizzes, surveys, and polls as well as collect multiple responses and view them in real time. You can add multimedia images to a survey or quiz to make it more interactive and engaging.

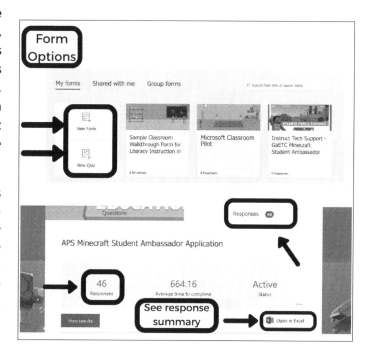

GREAT BECAUSE students can quickly answer questions. Then you can display the responses on a screen or whiteboard. These responses can begin a discussion or help you determine how to modify your teaching.

SETUP IS INTERMEDIATE.
Populate the form with questions before you begin your lesson. Once you create your form, you can share it with students using a QR code, or in OneNote, PowerPoint, or Teams.

Access Forms from the web at **forms.office.com**, and sign in with your Office 365 school account. Click on **My Forms**, and select either **new form** or **new quiz** to begin creating. Name your form or quiz, and begin to add your questions.

ALLOWS YOU TO check for student understanding. Collect student responses and use the information to differentiate your upcoming instruction. Try taking the responses and throwing them into a word cloud such as Wordle (wordle.net). This can kick off a class discussion or a fun activity called **Philosophical Chairs.**

GIVES THIS INFORMATION Forms creates a spreadsheet that displays comparative student data. You also can see the data displayed graphically. Simply go to the "Responses" section of the form to create a spreadsheet, and the data will auto-populate.

Microsoft Forms provides information such as the average time it took to complete the form, as well as the individual or group results. Forms also provides the email of the person who took the assessment if you select this option.

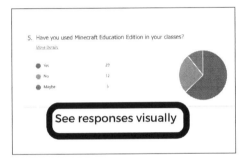

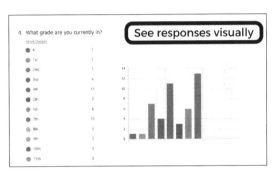

IDEAS

- Create Exit Tickets—short check-ins at the end of a lesson.
- Construct questions using the branching feature that take students down a path based on their answers. Based on the path, we can gather important information about their individual learning and understanding and see them as unique learners.
- Attach Forms to lessons or videos for student feedback.

WHAT'S GREAT IS THAT you can share the results with your students so they can keep track of their own growth.

In quiz mode, you can add answers and scores. You can also add math-specific questions and equations. Additionally, Microsoft Forms now has the Immersive Reader built in to help struggling readers and English language learner (ELL) students more easily read the questions and prompts that are included.

SHOWS YOU THE INFORMATION IN THIS WAY: You can see responses for individuals as well as an overall summary report. Forms results can be exported to an Excel document or visualized in a chart or graph.

PEAR DECK

ACCESS FROM ANY DEVICE: peardeck.com

WHAT IS PEAR DECK? Pear Deck is a tool you add to PowerPoint that helps teachers layer on formative tasks that provide insight into how students are doing with comprehension of content and ideas. Teachers can go beyond simply static, informational slides, and create Interactive PowerPoints that let every student show their understanding by responding to questions or prompts.

GREAT BECAUSE you can engage students in their learning during those times of needed direct instruction. Simply add Pear Deck to an already made PowerPoint presentation. It can also be used with or without the teacher by using the student-paced lesson feature.

SET UP IS EASY. Here is how:

- Head to the Insert tool in PowerPoint.
- Once selected, head all the way to the end of the bar and you will find the "Add-in" feature on the PowerPoint toolbar.
- Select Add-in and search for Pear Deck and then add.
- Once you have added the tool, select the round Pear Deck Icon that will populate on the toolbar.
- Pear Deck will then populate on the right hand of the slides as shown below.
- Simply find the type of assessment slide you want to layer on to your deck and add any customized information. You can use a pre-made template or create your own custom interactive slide.

This sidebar will appear once the Pear Deck Add-in is installed.
Click around and check out all of the different templates and question tyes.

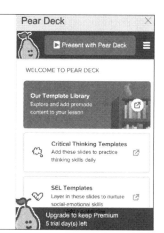

ALLOWS YOU TO ... add interactive elements to each slide by choosing to add text, choice, number options, push out web content, allow students to draw or have them drag content to the right place.

GIVES THIS INFORMATION: On the teacher dashboard, you can view all of the responses students have entered into Pear Deck. Teachers can choose to keep this information private or share it with the entire class by projecting the answers on the screen. You can also go back later to look more closely at how each student responded.

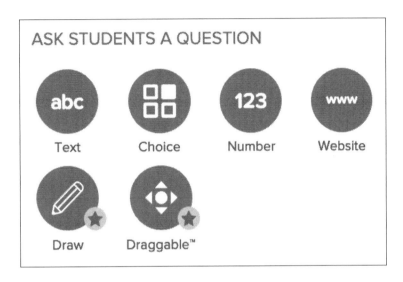

WHAT'S GREAT IS THAT students can access Pear Deck very easily. They use a code that is displayed by the teacher. Students head to joinpd.com on their device and use the code to get started. It is very easy and super engaging for students. They can also join through a QR code when needed.

SHOWS YOU THE INFORMATION privately on your teacher dashboard. You can also return any time to the PowerPoint to more purposefully look at student responses and use that information to inform future instruction. At any point in the lesson you can share student responses to have them comment or provide them the space to think about their own answers as they compare with those of the entire class. This process is known as metacognition and is a very important teaching strategy.

Check out **infused.link/peardecktips** for short tutorial videos.

IDEAS

- Illustrate learning! Have students use the drawing feature to solve a math problem or draw the inside of a cell.

- **Wrap it up!** Use the "End of lesson" template to have students do a brain dump or exit card at the end of a lesson.

- **Teach self-evaluation!** Use the thumb up and down feature to ask students how well they have comprehended a difficult piece of information or concept.

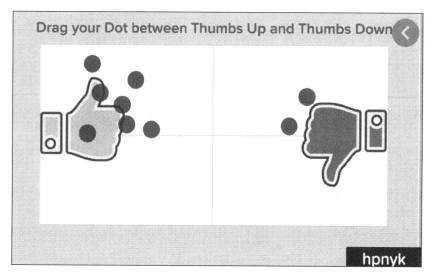

- Newsela, a site that provides authentic reading content, and Pear Deck have teamed up to create Daily Decks designed to spark student engagement! Each one features an adaptive news article with interactive prompts to get EVERY student learning. Learn more here. **infused.link/pearnews**.

- Create your own interactive content by using the fun draggable slide templates or create your own as you begin to master this amazing tool.

- For ninety days of the upgraded version and a chance to win one year, check out this link **peardeck.com/holly-clark**.

SEESAW

@HollyClarkEdu

WHAT IS SEESAW? Seesaw is a digital learning journal. It can be accessed from any device with online access at **web.seesaw.me,** and it should be a critical and well-used learning tool in any INFUSED Classroom.

Seesaw is a very simple way for students to record and share what's happening as they progress through the learning process using the six powerful tools: *photo, drawing, video, upload, notes,* and *adding a link.*

GREAT BECAUSE Seesaw gives students a place to document their learning, be creative, collaborate, and learn to use technology. They can add both verbal and graphical checks for understanding to their journal by using videos, photos, voice recordings, drawings, and more.

These checks can be shared out to the class on the class journal so that students have an opportunity to make their thinking visible and begin learning from each other through these more dynamic and powerful versions of formative assessments.

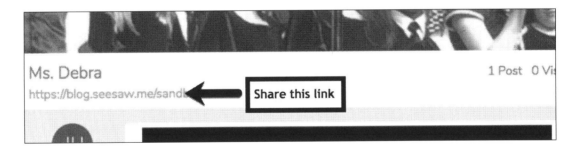

SETUP IS EASY. Create your classes, and invite students using a class code or QR code.

STUDENTS TURN IN WORK BY Adding responses (using one of the six tools: *photo, drawing, video, upload, notes,* or *link*) and then selecting the green checkmark on the top right corner of the screen. They can organize their checks for understanding into folders if the teacher makes them in advance.

ALLOWS YOU TO make all student thinking and learning visible in your classroom. Even if students are working from a worksheet, have them take a picture of it, then use the *record* button to tell exactly what they know or have learned.

 You can also use the Activity Library to find example lessons or watch webinars through their "PD in your PJs" series: **seesaw.me/professional-development**.

WHAT IS GREAT IS THAT students can share their creations with other students, expanding the learning happening in the room—because **students learn best from each other**. Hearing their classmates' responses enables them to fill in gaps in their own learning or discover that they might have missed some important information. They might even discover where they are excelling and get to know themselves better as learners.

The classroom-to-family connection is powerful. Seesaw allows you to send invitations home to family members to connect with your classroom. When they accept, families can be notified via app notifications, email, or text when their students add any new posts.

All data are safe and secure, and families are only notified about their own child's work. The teacher also can control which posts are shared with families.

SHOWS YOU INFORMATION in a chronological timeline when looking at posts through the journal view. You can also breadcrumb down to see posts by date and student only, making it easier to view student work more quickly. See the video at **infused.link/seesaw1** for more information.

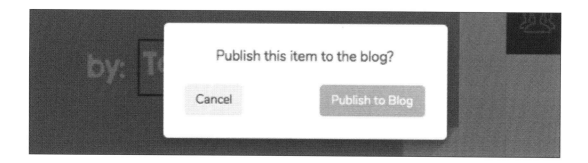

IDEAS

- Take pictures of students' "analog" creations where they can add drawings, add text, and record their voice to provide more understanding of their learning experience.

- Enhance learning by adding voice reflections, drawing on, or adding text to a picture already saved on the device. Or insert a picture or video that was created in another app or saved on your desktop or OneDrive.

- Insert a file from your computer and annotate, caption, or record over it.

ONENOTE

ACCESS FROM ANY DEVICE: onenote.office.com

WHAT IS ONENOTE? OneNote allows students to create really powerful digital notebooks that are accessible across all of your devices. These notebooks can be used over time as formative assessments that track student learning and understanding.

GREAT BECAUSE OneNote helps students stay organized in a digital world, eliminating the need for massive amounts of paper. They can also easily collaborate with their classmates within the notebooks.

Most importantly, they can keep track of their own learning and growth throughout a unit or the school year. This empowers them to understand themselves better as learners.

SETUP IS EASY. OneNote is free and can be easily accessed from all student devices. It is simple for students to locate and use this tool on a Windows 10 device by clicking on the start window and then the OneNote tile. It also can be accessed on any device by logging into the Microsoft portal through **office.com**.

ALLOWS STUDENTS TO showcase their learning by creating different notebooks for different projects. They can arrange their thinking in sections and pages, just like a traditional student notebook or binder, but use all of the rich media tools of a connected device. Students are also able to seamlessly work together on projects and other classroom assignments. They also can create a notebook for sketchnotes to enhance their construction of knowledge.

GIVES YOU THIS INFORMATION with a shared notebook, the teacher gets a glimpse into the learning patterns of their students. This reflective process enables teachers to provide meaningful feedback and inform their own practice.

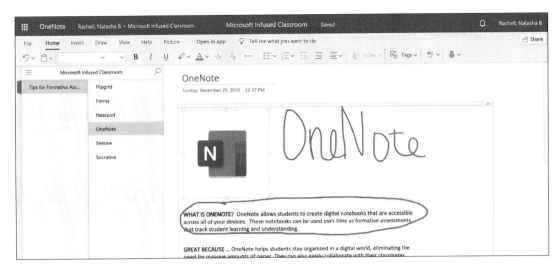

SHOWS YOU THE INFORMATION arranged in notebooks, sections, and pages, but it is not limited by this. Students can supercharge their learning with the addition of thinking routines, sketchnotes, attachments, videos, images, and rich media. To fit any organizational style, they personalize their notebooks to meet their individual learning needs.

WHAT'S GREAT IS THAT OneNote notebooks are automatically saved to your OneDrive account in the cloud so students can pick up where they left off in the classroom, at home, or in transit.

IDEAS

- Create a Notebook to formatively assess primary students with reading fluency. Students can use the recording feature to record their reading over time.

- Annotate over text to show an evolving understanding of key ideas. For example, underline and highlight parts of speech and comment on word choice, plot, character, and theme. This annotation practice works for classes from Advanced Placement (AP) to Advancement via Individual Determination (AVID).

- Create unit-based learning journals that show student learning over time in multiple subjects. Insert images and video from class activities such as lab experiments. These journals can be easily assessed with a quick look and feedback.

FLIPGRID

ACCESS FROM ANY DEVICE: flipgrid.com

WHAT IS FLIPGRID? Flipgrid is a video-response platform featuring grids and topics. Each grid is populated with topics, and the topic is where students leave their video responses or upload content. Topics empower teachers to ask different discussion questions or post prompts based on the overarching subject of the grid.

GREAT BECAUSE teachers can create really quick and easy checks for understanding. Even the students who are shy or slow to respond or don't typically raise their hands have an opportunity to participate with Flipgrid. It works great for students who just need a bit more time to process before they post. It also allows students to build articulate verbal reasoning skills as they post and respond. Video responses often prompt further discussions among students in the class.

Flipgrid is quick and easy to use, so when you know you need to do a quick check for understanding but you don't have anything prepared, you can make a grid on the fly.

SETUP IS EASY. You just choose one of the three types of grids, name the grid, make a topic to ask a question, and let the video responses begin. For example, name a grid "The Outsiders," and ask questions about the book through topics within that grid.

ALLOWS STUDENTS TO show, reflect, and comment on exactly where they are in the learning process. Students can record videos in as little as fifteen seconds or as long as five minutes. They can watch other student videos and compare these with their own responses and learning. This allows students to "think about thinking" as they listen to how other students responded to the same prompt.

GIVES YOU THE INFORMATION IN THIS WAY: Your students create video responses on a grid that can be seen by those who have access to that grid. Their best thinking or examples can be added to a mixtape to show growth over time.

WHAT IS GREAT IS THAT Flipgrid allows you to collaborate with other classrooms by using the *GridPals* option at the top of the dashboard. It also has a fantastic *Disco Library* to help spark lesson ideas. It teaches students the digital citizenship lessons of effectively commenting and communicating with others via video and media. (Note: teachers need to spend a bit of time at first talking about proper commenting and meaningful replies.)

SHOWS YOU THE INFORMATION in an organized grid, which makes it highly visual, easy to navigate, and easy to access. From the student view, the videos even play "Netflix style"—one after the other, making them easy to watch. Even better, valuable feedback can be added from the teacher view.

 Check out *Fliphunts*, an engaging digital scavenger hunt created by Kathi Kersznowski: **blog.flipgrid.com/news/fliphunt**.

IDEAS

- **Science**—Students take time-lapse videos of science projects and upload those to a grid. They can use the comment feature to explain what happened during the process and briefly analyze the results.

- **Art**—Students give their interpretations of an art piece. Then have them listen to the other student interpretations, reflecting on why they might be dramatically different or even the same.

- **Language Arts**—Students explain their comprehension after reading a chapter in a book. Have students use Flipgrid to brainstorm possible writing ideas for their next writing unit.

- **All Subjects**—*Private Student Grids*: During a unit of study, students track their learning over time on this private grid. They can respond to questions, ask their own, or even reflect on what they notice about their own learning strengths. Teachers can use this to assess learning for that individual student over time.

JOIN THE FLIPGRID FREE ONLINE COURSE at **infused.link/online**

SOCRATIVE

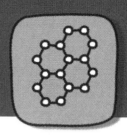

@HollyClarkEdu

WHAT IS SOCRATIVE? Socrative is a website and app that allows you to quickly gather information about your students' learning in the form of closed and open-ended questions. There is also a game-like response area called "Space Race." For our purposes, we will discuss the Quick Question option. This option is one of the choices found on the app's Launchpad or front page: **socrative.com**.

GREAT BECAUSE it allows you to hear from every student in your class, not just the few who raise their hands to answer questions. You can use the *Quick Question* option to do a quick Check for Understanding that will illuminate in a short amount of time what the students have learned.

SETUP IS EASY. The website's interface is simple, and you can navigate it without prior setup.

ALLOWS YOU TO make all of your students' thinking visible by asking an open-ended question. You can gather student responses in one stream, then keep and dissect responses later for further data.

GIVES YOU THIS INFORMATION Students' answers appear on the screen, allowing them to compare their responses with their peers' as they finish. Plus, Socrative gives you access to a saved copy of your class's responses for later and saves it using Excel, so you can do a lot of manipulation of student data.

WHAT'S GREAT IS THAT students enter a state of metacognition as they think about one another's answers in comparison with their own, prompting them to continue learning even after they've responded. This tool also allows students to vote on the best answer from everyone's responses.

SHOWS YOU THE INFORMATION in a simple stream. Socrative's interactive approach is fun and chock-full of important data.

IDEAS

- **Math**—Have students tell you in their own words how they would solve a math problem. This addresses Common Core standards that ask students to explain how they would solve a math problem.

- **Language Arts**—Doing a response to literature? Have students share out their thesis statements. This way they can see one another's ideas, and you can gauge where they are in the process.

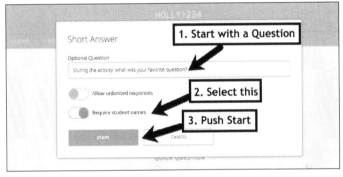

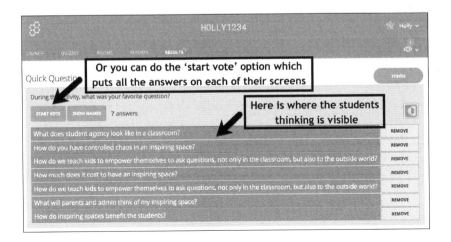

Differentiation

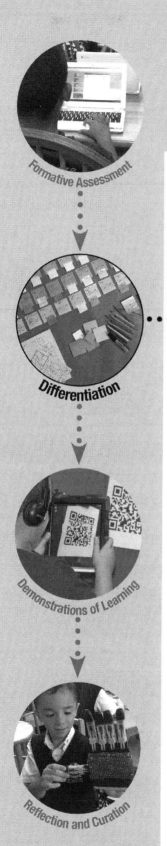

Formative Assessment

Differentiation

Demonstrations of Learning

Reflection and Curation

Now that you have done some formative assessment, hopefully you have gathered some important data about each of your students. Using the Understanding by Design (UbD) framework, you'll be able to use those data to design instruction that helps each individual student meet the learning goal. It's time to take those data, analyze them, and uncover where students might be struggling, where they can jump ahead, and where they might need some additional resources. And what you're likely to discover is that your students are heading down the path of growth in very different ways.

Differentiation is crucial in learning. It recognizes the reality that everyone learns differently and that each child possesses unique learning abilities. The goal for us as educators is to teach to those strengths, not to the class as a whole. Simply put, differentiation is defined as the delivery model of instruction that best meets the needs of every student in the classroom.

Differentiation is a multidimensional and sometimes difficult concept to employ in traditional classroom settings. However, the tools and technology we'll discuss in this section will provide you a few examples of how you can use differentiation to amplify the learning process.

Differentiation, as described by Susan Allan Demirsky and Carol Ann Tomlinson in their book *Leadership for Differentiating Schools and Classrooms*, is guided by three principles:

1. Respectful tasks that are inclusive of each child's learning style

2. Flexible grouping, in which a student is grouped with peers who bring out the best in that child's learning experience and where a collaborative environment can flourish

3. Continued assessment and adjustment of instruction by the teacher

This section explores technology that allows you to deliver respectful tasks that are inclusive of each child's learning strengths. By using the tools in this section, you will be able to provide each of your students with the resources that will better equip them to make meaning of the content.

For example, ask yourself

- How do my students learn best?
- Would they most benefit from watching a video about the concept on their own so they can pause it and write down notes?
- Would reading about the lesson be helpful?
- Would a visual prompt such as a concept map or picture help some of my students make sense of what they are learning?
- Would allowing some of my students to sketchnote concepts and ideas help?
- How can I best know where they are in the learning process? Have I used the tools from the previous section to do this effectively?

The tools in the section will provide a way for you to easily deliver these differentiated resources to your students.

Strategy

Use the information you have gathered from formative assessments to decide where the students are in the learning process.

Next, curate or create resources that would help that individual learner's needs. When done well, these resources will allow students to construct knowledge and empower their learning.

Finally, decide which platform you'll use to pass out the resources. (We've provided a few great examples on the next pages.) These tools will help you differentiate the resources in a place your students can effortlessly access as needed.

Tools:

OneNote

Teams

Microsoft Learning Tools

IMMERSIVE READER

WHAT IS IMMERSIVE READER? Microsoft's Immersive Reader is a full-screen reading experience to increase the readability of content by providing a real-time read-aloud of any typed print or image.

GREAT BECAUSE it helps students with dysgraphia and dyslexia, but it can help anyone who wants to increase their fluency or needs help decoding more complex texts. Immersive Reader implements proven techniques to improve reading and writing for students regardless of their age or ability.

SETUP IS EASY. Look for the Immersive Reader icon embedded within a platform for instant access or use through other applications such as Office Lens or Microsoft Word.

ALLOWS YOU TO automatically read and highlight text. Text can be read aloud to students or they may select individual words to be pronounced in English or translated to the language of their choice. Students are able to highlight lines, change font colors, and edit text size—all to best fit their individual needs.

GIVES YOU THIS INFORMATION Immersive Reader creates an instant read-aloud version of text and can translate the text into over sixty languages.

WHAT'S GREAT IS THAT Special grammar options allow students to toggle between highlighting nouns, verbs, adjectives, and adverbs or even to break words down into syllables. Immersive Reader can act as a support system for emerging readers or be a lifeline for students learning English.

SHOWS YOU THE INFORMATION IN THIS WAY: It gives students access to a picture dictionary and audio definitions. All of the changes that students make to a text selection are specifically for their own viewing, and they do not alter the text for other students.

IDEAS

- Writing—After students have completed a writing task, have them use Immersive Reader embedded in Word to listen to what they've written, and use it to independently make edits.

- For more information see **infused.link/techquity**.

ONENOTE HYPERDOC

ACCESS FROM ANY DEVICE: onenote.office.com

@apsitnatasha

WHAT IS A ONENOTE HYPERDOC? A HyperDoc is a student-facing digital lesson plan you create and package using OneNote. When curating resources for a HyperDoc, the emphasis is on pedagogy and meeting individual student needs.

GREAT BECAUSE an entire digital resource document or notebook can be created for students to access all content in one place.

A OneNote HyperDoc provides a structure for students to stay organized and on task. Students develop agency by making choices as they progress through the lesson. Within the HyperDoc, students can work collaboratively or alone.

SETUP IS INTERMEDIATE. HyperDocs rely on knowledge of pedagogy to create this new type of blended learning experience.

To set up a HyperDoc using OneNote:

- Include all four Cs—Collaboration, Creativity, Communication, and Critical Thinking as part of the lesson design.
- Create a structured document with links to resources that allow students to explore and apply their learning.
- Use the HyperDoc templates provided at **hyperdocs.co.**
- Organize the flow of the lesson using sections.
- Type, write, or audio record notes for your students, or allow them to do the same.
- Tag and prioritize ideas in the HyperDoc.
- Include content such as images, text, audio, and video and allow them to respond in the HyperDoc by doing the same.
- Sync any lesson notes across multiple devices.

ALLOWS YOU TO quickly organize and create student-facing lessons that can be accessed at every learning level. Curate multimedia resources, organize the flow of a lesson in one place, and guide students through the process of making their learning visible. In a well-crafted lesson, HyperDocs include blended learning strategies, self-paced learning, and differentiation.

GIVES YOU THIS INFORMATION Using Class Notebooks, teachers are able to easily see each student's notebook and can easily disseminate information to each student based on their needs.

WHAT'S GREAT IS THAT HyperDocs created in OneNote are ideal for all students, no matter their learning style or need. Students can add images, audio, text, diagrams, videos, and more to capture their learning in a way that best meets their needs. Students also can use OneNote's Immersive Reader feature to better access directions and ideas if needed.

SHOWS YOU THE INFORMATION in a clear, appealing, and logically organized digital or visit the Wakelet Collection of our favorite HyperDocs **infused.link/hyperdocs** page.

> **More Ideas:** Visit **HyperDoc.co** or join their very active Facebook group at **facebook.com/groups/hyperdocs**.

Did you know? Links in a OneNote that take students to resources for consumption of information only is called a Text Set. A HyperDoc is so much more than this. Check out the graphic below to better understand the difference between the two.

Text Sets → HyperDocs

YOU ARE HERE

Multimedia Text Sets...	HyperDocs...
Are a doc with links to a variety of media on a given topic for students to consume information.	Are a *digital lesson* with links to a variety of media on a given topic for students to consume information *and include one or more opportunities for students to connect beyond the classroom, collaborate, create (or show what they know), share, reflect, and/or incorporate extension activities.*
Provide opportunities for exploration of a topic.	Provide opportunities for exploration of a topic *and include multiple parts of a lesson plan all packaged in one place. Activities are self-paced or delivered in a flexible blended learning environment, differentiated with extensions and benefits of flipped classrooms to meet the needs of all students, and equip educational communities with distance learning for building inclusion.*
Build background knowledge and help with comprehension during lessons on the topic.	Build background knowledge and help with comprehension during lessons on the topic. *Package pre-teaching, teaching, and extensions for scaffolding lessons.*
Inquiry-based, offer choice, differentiated,	Inquiry-based, offer choice, differentiated, - *include accountability for formative assessment. Creators deliberately choose web tools to give students opportunities to Engage • Explore • Explain • Apply • Share • Reflect • Extend the learning*
A place to offload your lecture	A place to offload your lecture *and reimagine various ways to redefine the student learning experience. (referring to the R in the SAMR model)*
A chance to move around and confer with students -- more face time!	A chance to move around and confer with students -- more face time! *Teacher and peers provide immediate feedback and personalize instruction seamlessly.*

TEAMS

ACCESS FROM ANY DEVICE: teams.office.com

WHAT IS TEAMS? Teams is a chat-based collaboration tool that gives students and teachers the ability to work together and share information in a common space.

GREAT BECAUSE it is the hub where students can actively connect and collaborate in real time to complete differentiated tasks.

SETUP IS MODERATE. Create a Team, and then either add students ahead of time or invite them using a code. Create additional channels to allow for easy differentiation by assigning certain students to each.

ALLOWS YOU TO create differentiated groups based on student needs; have conversations and share feedback with students while organizing and tracking group assignments and student progress.

GIVES YOU THIS INFORMATION Teams allows teachers to collect information through assignments and real-time conversations with students, while also allowing room to embed videos, apps, and resources directly within the space.

WHAT'S GREAT IS THAT it allows you to differentiate student learning through the different application integrations and to organize resources and related material. Teachers can customize the learning experience with OneNote Class Notebooks to share notes and files and give feedback to individual students based on their respective needs.

SHOWS YOU THE INFORMATION IN THIS WAY: Teams has a menu layout with buttons along the side and tabs across the top to keep assignments, chats, and activities organized and easy to find. Teachers can review student-submitted material simply by scrolling through each assignment, reviewing and commenting along the way.

IDEAS

- Place your guided reading groups in Teams for quick and easy differentiation.

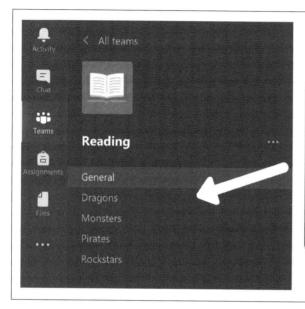

Create individual "channels" for your guided reading groups for easy differentiation

- Working on research projects? Create channels for each topic and assign students to the appropriate channel.

- Book Clubs: Create a "secret" chat in which the teacher assigns certain students to a Teams channel, and the group discusses a book based on reading levels and interests.

MICROSOFT LEARNING TOOLS

GET MORE MICROSOFT LEARNING TOOLS IDEAS AND RESOURCES, HEAD TO
infused.link/mswakelet
infused.link/msaccessibility

Felisa Ford

WHAT ARE MICROSOFT LEARNING TOOLS? Microsoft Learning Tools are free and inclusive reading, writing, communication, and math tools designed to personalize learning for students. Learning tools help make it easier for students to demonstrate their learning and make their thinking visible by making the content accessible to all students.

Learn more about how you can meet the needs of diverse learners: **infused.link/mslearnmore**

GREAT BECAUSE learning tools help improve reading, strengthen writing, enhance communication and math understanding, and optimize class time. Students can synthesize the content in a variety of creative ways, such as a Think-Pic-Share representation of their learning, which makes it easier for them to demonstrate their understanding. Through tools such as the Immersive Reader teachers can help students improve reading. Students take ownership of their own learning and have the tools to make their thinking visible.

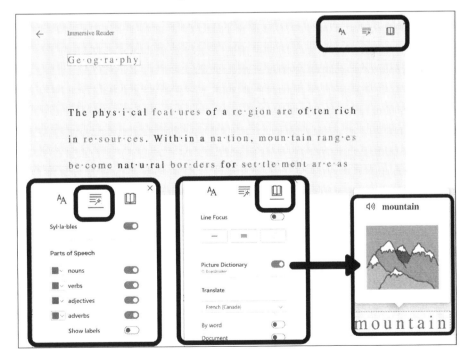

To learn more about Microsoft Learning Tools, visit the Microsoft Education Blog: **infused.link/mslearningtools**.

For more information on Think-Pic-Share go to: **infused.link/thinkpicshare**.

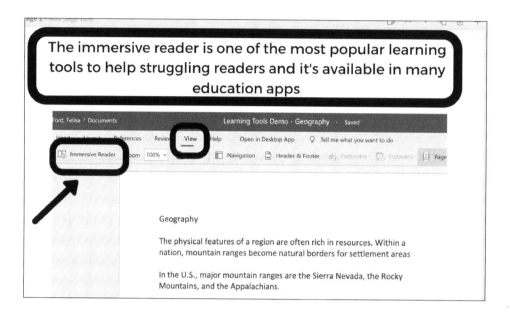

SETUP IS EASY. Learning tools are already embedded inside of Microsoft Tools and apps.

ALLOWS YOU TO improve reading, strengthen writing, and make the best use of classroom time. The Math Assistant in OneNote also has practice and differentiation tools for math.

GIVES YOU THIS INFORMATION by providing Tools provide students with the option to use grammar tools, identify parts of speech, translate words or documents, use a picture dictionary, and choose the preferred voice for the read-aloud feature. This helps teachers differentiate content to further help each student based on their needs and what tool will help them attain success.

WHAT'S GREAT IS THAT learning tools offer an extra layer of support and reduce unnecessary distractions for students so they can focus on the text. Students maximize their learning experience by highlighting words, increasing and decreasing speed, font size, and spacing, changing page color, turning syllables on, highlighting parts of speech, turning on line focus, and using the picture dictionary.

Watch these videos to see how Microsoft Learning Tools support students with dyslexia: **infused.link/dyslexia** and **infused.link/dyslexia1**

SHOWS YOU THE INFORMATION in Microsoft platforms by clicking "View" and then "Learning Tools" or "Immersive Reader." The features and functions of the Learning Tools are experienced in the same manner across the desktop, web, or app so that student access to the content remains consistent and at the center of learning.

IDEAS

- Use Immersive Reader within OneNote to assist students with reading fluency. Type sight words into OneNote and have students use the Immersive Reader Learning Tool to listen to words read aloud, repeating them for automaticity.

- Use the Read-Aloud feature to help struggling readers better understand content, practice reading, and understand instructions and directions for an assignment.

- Use Picture Dictionary and Syllabication to help students learn new vocabulary words and pronunciation.

- Struggling writers can use the Dictate function to overcome writer's block to author text. Students can combine the Dictate tool with the Editor tool in Word to write research papers and use the read-aloud feature to revise, edit, and proofread their work.

- Use the "Translate" feature in the Learning Tools so that ELL students are able to ask questions and communicate with their teacher and other students.

- The Math Assistant can support students with independent math practice at home, especially students who struggle with word problems. The read-aloud component can help struggling readers as well as guide them through the steps needed to solve math equations.

Demonstrations
OF LEARNING

Formative Assessment

Differentiation

Demonstrations of Learning

Reflection and Curation

Up to this point, we've discussed the value of gathering information through formative assessments and using those data to differentiate learning. We've explored ways to provide each child with "respectful tasks" and resources that will help them move closer to their learning goals. It's now time to empower students to show both their "transfer of learning" and how they made meaning of the content. In other words, it's time for students to demonstrate their learning.

To ensure that students create meaningful demonstrations of learning, the methods they use must be multifaceted and layered. Thankfully, technology allows students to demonstrate their learning in authentic and rich ways. It provides us with the opportunity to hear from every student, uncover their thinking, visualize the steps they took and the applications they made, and understand the metacognition behind the experience. Technology makes it possible to take something that was once one-dimensional, such as a poster, and layer it with student voice, explanations, and even virtual reality to make their learning come to life. The result is that learning becomes much more meaningful and interesting in the process. In the following pages, we will give you an overview of the technology tools that make it fun and easy to allow for a variety of demonstrations of student learning.

In each type of demonstration of learning, students start with a question that is built around a learning target. Then students construct knowledge, keep a record of their journey, and show their learning in a digitally rich product.

> "Understanding is revealed when students make sense of and transfer their learning through authentic performance."
>
> **— McTighe and Wiggins, Understanding by Design**

What do you grade? You grade growth!

Evaluate their growth toward the learning target, not the fonts they used, the number of pages, the number of questions they got right, or the mistakes they made along the way.

Strategy

FIRST, allow students the choice to respond in a way that fits their learning style. Make sure they are aware of the learning target toward which they are trying to show growth. Show them exemplars from other students if you have them—or examples you have curated from other sources.

NEXT, if it is something that fits their learning style, let them use one of the ten tools we will cover in this section. They might do a screencast, a video, or even a visual story or Minecraft project.

FINALLY, allow them the opportunity to keep these demonstrations of learning in a portfolio or digital binder such as OneNote where they can start to curate their learning journey. Being able to see growth over time is powerful not only to the teacher but to the student as well.

Demonstrations of Learning
STUDENT PUBLISHING

Demonstrations of Learning refers to a wide range of artifacts that allow students to exhibit what they have learned. These learning products provide students with the opportunity to show they have met certain learning goals or targets. If designed correctly, these demonstrations should provide the teacher with rich information about student learning and growth, far beyond what can be gleaned from standard multiple-choice questions or worksheets. This section provides examples of the different activities and tools students can use to show their learning with the visual elements that make it more dynamic and rich.

WHY WE DO THIS: We encourage students to publish their work so that they become authors, developing their reading and writing skills by honing the digital literacies they need. They can do this by creating for and sharing with an authentic audience. Students take ownership of the process by keeping track of their ideas in one place, creating reflection of understanding journals, and creating and publishing pieces that will demonstrate their learning and growth over time. Students of any age in any subject area can easily publish writing. They can create digital books, using OneNote for a more private option and Spark Page for a more public-facing option.

HOW STUDENT PUBLISHING MAKES STUDENT THINKING VISIBLE: Digital books and journals prompt students to compile the many stages of their learning in a single location. They can add graphics, videos, and sound recordings, and they can talk out their ideas and thinking using the recording function, so that we can better understand them as learners.

HOW DIGITAL PUBLISHING GIVES STUDENTS A VOICE: When students have a place to gather their thinking, such as in a digital book or journal, they create a collection of work that can help them better understand who they are as learners. What's more, as a creative tool, digital publishing gives each student a platform to develop their voice, as both a learner and a writer.

HOW DIGITAL PUBLISHING ALLOWS STUDENTS TO SHOW THEIR WORK: Students can publish their work using Flipgrid Shorts or Sway (see listing to follow).

WHAT STUDENTS CAN CREATE: All kinds of digital books, including a collaborative global book with schools from across the globe! They could do this in OneNote, Teams, or Book Creator.

YOU COULD TRY: Task them with creating science or math journals, interactive stories, research journals, and science writeups. Book Creator would make a good place to start.

OR EVEN: They could develop Adobe Spark Page of sentence starters, how-to books, and photo books. They can even create collaborative class anthologies that focus on a unit of study with blackout poetry or poetry journals, using OneNote or Seesaw.

AND FOR THE TEACHER: Create differentiated instructional books for your learners, using OneNote.

> "If students are sharing their work with the world, they want it to be good. If they're just sharing it with you, they want it good enough."
>
> – Rushton Hurley

BOOK CREATOR

ACCESS BY GOING TO: app.bookcreator.com

WHAT IS BOOK CREATOR? Book Creator is a web based application that allows students to create books, comics, journals, and authentic learning artifacts, which they can then publish online for others to view and read. This is one of the best creation apps out there and should be used in the classroom often!

GREAT BECAUSE it allows students to easily publish their work.

SET UP IS EASY. Students simply sign in to Book Creator using their Office 365 account. Book Creator can be easily accessed using the Edge Browser or added to Teams.

STUDENTS TURN IN WORK BY publishing to your private class bookshelf within the Book Creator app or link to it in Teams. They can draft the work in Microsoft Word and showcase the work in their own book using Book Creator. They can even upload and save in Office 365 when needed. Students can also print their book or publish it online and using the link provided, share it with others.

ALLOWS STUDENTS TO work independently and collaboratively to create digital books and learning journals. Students simply choose a book type and shape, then use the add button in the upper left corner to important many different media elements, photos, videos, text, create drawings or add their own voice recordings. They can creatively add color and backgrounds to make their books look more professional. They can even combine their book with a classmate to make a more robust book.

SHOWS YOU INFORMATION IN THIS WAY: Students and teachers can view their book or journal on the Book Creator website, share it via social media, or link to it on their personal web page.

For more ideas on Book Creator visit **infused.link/bookcreator**.

IDEAS

- Have students create a comic book of the Water Cycle or events of the Civil War.

- Students can create a narrative writing assignment using the comic book option. Have them use a cartoon creator app to add fun cartoon images to their books.

- Have students create their own writing journals. They can even use the record feature to make their own audio books or illustrate their own work by using the drawing tools.

ON A VACATION, A GIRL WAS PRESSURED INTO SNOWBOARDING DOWN A DANGEROUS HILL WHICH WAS SEVEN MILES FROM HER HOTEL AND ANY PEOPLE WHATSOEVER.
OKAY, I'M READY...
I CAN DO THIS...
WHEW, I MADE IT.
HER FAITHFUL DOG WILLOW CAME ALL THAT WAY TO WARN HER... MAYBE SHE WOULD GAIN HER RESPECT.

ADOBE SPARK PAGE

ACCESS FROM ANY DEVICE: spark.adobe.com

Tanya Avrith

WHAT IS ADOBE SPARK PAGE? Adobe Spark Page lets students show what they know by creating modern, professional, and attention-grabbing web stories that combine text and graphics. An interactive multimedia tool, it can replace the traditional research report for students in middle and high school.

GREAT BECAUSE it makes thinking visible. Students can demonstrate their learning using images, videos, words, and links. They use their own images or access and share high-quality free images available within the app. Spark Page allows students to publish a dynamic and complex multimedia story.

Students also can personalize the visual look and feel of their work. To learn more, watch the following videos: **infused.link/sparkbranding** and **infused.link/sparkbranding2**.

SETUP IS INTERMEDIATE. Once the school or district has access to the free EDU accounts, the students will have access to their accounts and all of the features of the tool: **infused.link/sparklogin**.

Note: The school accounts adhere to American federal privacy laws and are Family Educational Rights and Privacy Act (FERPA) and Children's Online Privacy Protection Rule (COPPA) compliant. Students simply log in using their school-issued account. Make sure this is set up first by having your school IT or leadership head over to **spark.adobe.com/edu**.

STUDENTS TURN IN WORK BY publishing a shareable link in an email, to a class website, or on a social media outlet. They will then use the link to turn in the finished artifact using a curation tool such as Padlet or Wakelet, or they can share with the link in their OneNote or Classroom Teams: **infused.link/sparkpage**.

ALLOWS STUDENTS TO create visually engaging websites that add context to their research and writing. This revolutionizes the traditional writing assignment, taking one-dimensional stories and turning them into multidimensional visual narratives published for a wider audience.

Students can use their Page to curate screenshots or pictures they have taken of their creations (both analog and digital) to demonstrate growth of their learning.

WHAT'S GREAT IS THAT Adobe Spark Page is simple to use, but the published product looks sophisticated and professional. Students can work independently or collaborate with other classmates.

Check out Adobe's Edex community, where you will find many tutorials and lesson ideas here: **edex.adobe.com/spark**.

SHOWS YOU THE INFORMATION IN THIS WAY: When published, students are provided with a unique URL that they can share as a web page. This can be scrolled through for information the way any web page operates. Students can also use feedback to edit their work or download it as a PDF.

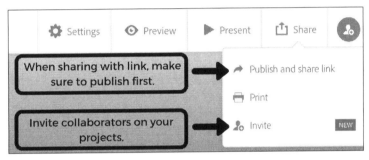

IDEAS

- **Social Studies**—Have students choose a historic era and create an interactive timeline complete with narratives, images, videos, and sound bites to bring the period to life.

- **Language Arts**—Have students compose a personal narrative combining their images and images they access within the application. Use spoken-word poetry and video news clips to add context to their story.

- **Science**—Have students perform an experiment and demonstrate their learning by creating a web page constructed with images, text, and research information to produce an interactive report project.

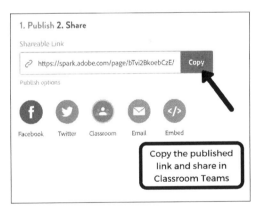

SWAY

ACCESS FROM ANY DEVICE: sway.office.com

WHAT IS SWAY? Sway is a resource that allows students to engage in digital storytelling by using digital media that showcases their understanding of content in a meaningful, visual way.

GREAT BECAUSE students are able to visualize their learning and tell the story of the content in a way that makes sense to them by including text, images, video, audio files, and other media.

SETUP IS EASY. Students can access Sway through **sway.com** or by clicking the Sway tile located in their Microsoft portal located at office.com. Because Sway is web-based, it can be accessed from any device.

STUDENTS TURN IN WORK BY sharing the link to their Sway directly with their teacher. A Sway also can be embedded into another Sway, or into another app such as OneNote, for example.

ALLOWS YOU TO start from scratch and personalize your presentation, start building your Sway from a topic in which the AI of Microsoft will build a template that serves as a starting point, or import a Word or PowerPoint document directly into Sway. If students import a Word or PowerPoint into Sway, Sway will format what it thinks the presentation should look like. Students are then able to use this as a starting point and make adjustments as needed. For more information on creating a Sway, visit **infused.link/howtosway**.

@apsitnatasha

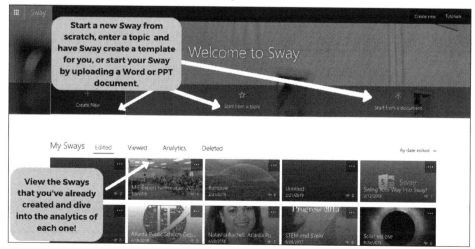

Start a new Sway from scratch, enter a topic and have Sway create a template for you, or start your Sway by uploading a Word or PPT document.

View the Sways that you've already created and dive into the analytics of each one!

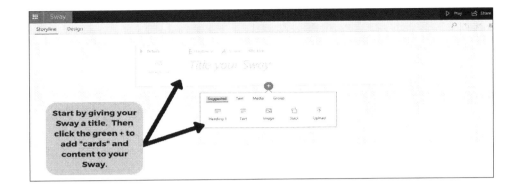

Start by giving your Sway a title. Then click the green + to add "cards" and content to your Sway.

WHAT'S GREAT IS THAT students can work independently, or easily collaborate on their digital storytelling projects, bringing the content to life.

SHOWS YOU THE INFORMATION IN THIS WAY: Play the presentation either vertically or horizontally, or by clicking the forward and backward arrows to manually advance to the next card of the Sway. Sways also can be looped and presented in autoplay.

IDEAS

- **For art classes**—Have students take photos of their projects and upload them into their own Sway to create a portfolio of their work and projects over the course of the class. You could also create a library of student work in a "Classroom Sway" and have all students upload photos for one particular assignment. This could become a shared digital art gallery.

- **For PE classes**—Have students take images of themselves performing different physical activities, showcasing proper technique and form, and upload them into their own individual Sway. Students also could include their data, such as distance, time, and progress, to showcase physical improvement throughout the year.

- **For science classes**—Students can create and publish their lab reports in a Sway. These digital stories include their data, images of their experiments, and the evidence that justifies their results.

- **Teacher Tip**—Want to learn more about digital storytelling with Sway? Head to the FREE Microsoft Educator Community (MEC) and take the "Digital Storytelling with Sway" course!

MINECRAFT: EDUCATION EDITION

WHAT IS MINECRAFT Education Edition? Minecraft Education Edition is the education edition of Microsoft's popular open-world game with an instructional focus. It promotes problem-based learning, helps teachers include the four Cs (Collaboration, Creativity, Critical Thinking, and Communication), and allows students to demonstrate their learning in a creative way.

Students can collaborate with peers and creatively demonstrate their learning in Minecraft

EXPLORE BIODIVERSITY IN MINECRAFT

Educators can join the community, get trained, and find lessons or challenges to engage students

GREAT BECAUSE it allows students to demonstrate their learning in a creative and authentic manner while working collaboratively to create standards-based projects. To see the power of MinecraftEDU, watch this student-created example from a mission project done by a fourth grader in California: **infused.link/minecraftexample**.

SETUP IS MODERATE. Minecraft Education Edition works on Windows 10, Mac, and iPad. It requires an Office 365 education account. It can be downloaded from the Minecraft Education Edition website: education.minecraft.net/get-started, Windows Store, or the Apple Store. Teachers can even have students join a class "world" with a shared code, or, if students are on the same network, they can join their peers' worlds.

STUDENTS TURN IN WORK BY multiple avenues. They can create student portfolios or document their work in the Book and Quill which allows students to create stories by allowing students to add screenshots/pictures taken with the Minecraft camera and then adding text to complete the story. Students can even screen record their creation (see **infused.link/minecraftrecorder** for more info on this) to screencast their creation—explaining what they learned and expanding on their decisions to demonstrate their learning. These items can be exported, saved, and shared outside of Minecraft: Education Edition to Microsoft Teams or OneNote.

GET MORE MINECRAFT EDUCATION EDITION IDEAS HERE:
infused.link/minecraftideas
infused.link/minecraftedu

ALLOWS STUDENTS TO collaborate, create, and demonstrate their understanding while in the high-interest world of Minecraft. Students are able to demonstrate and show evidence of their learning and capture that evidence through the use of a portfolio, book and quill, camera, or even better, a student-created and narrated screencast.

WHAT'S GREAT IS THAT Every Minecraft: Education Edition world includes an immersive reader that provides access for struggling readers and ELL students to understand learning objectives and to demonstrate their learning through the creative world of Minecraft. External resources can be added to Minecraft to support student learning, allowing students to make their thinking visible and amplifying their voices for peers, teachers, and parents in an authentic way that is unique to the student. Through limitless collaboration, Minecraft Education Edition helps amplify student voice as they view, edit, and build and showcase their creativity and design thinking. Students also can incorporate coding into Minecraft by using Code Builder, which is built into the platform.

GIVES YOU THE INFORMATION by showing students their work in block form. Students also can take screencasts of their work, as in the example of the mission previously mentioned: **infused.link/minecraftexample**.

IDEAS

There are many creative ways that Minecraft Education Edition can be used in the classroom.

- Pixel art of community helpers
- Create an interactive history timeline
- Create the cover of their favorite book
- Minecraft Build Challenges that encourage students to create builds based on a specific challenge theme, such as the Mission San Diego de Alcala challenge

Demonstrations of Learning
VISUAL STORYTELLING

2

WHY WE DO THIS: When we ask our learners to show us what they know using a visual medium, we're asking them to research, write, think critically, and carefully organize their understanding in a coherent, meaningful way. This type of demonstration of learning encourages students to apply higher-order thinking practices and develop their communication skills beyond the use of text and words.

HOW VISUAL STORYTELLING MAKES THINKING VISIBLE: It prompts students to tell a story through the combined use of words, images, and sounds.

HOW VISUAL STORYTELLING AMPLIFIES STUDENT VOICE: Visual storytelling provides a medium through which learners can show and narrate their understanding of concepts. Students add media elements to words or writing that can bring a more complex representation of the story to the page. This is an important skill for students to understand and be able to do in a modern world.

HOW VISUAL STORYTELLING ALLOWS STUDENTS TO SHARE THEIR WORK: Students can publish their creations to their Microsoft Sway presentation or Adobe Spark Page, their digital portfolio, a topic on Flipgrid, or share them via social media, thereby allowing an authentic audience to view their work.

WHAT STUDENTS CAN CREATE

YOU COULD TRY: Have students create documentaries based on their research, videos for book reviews, vocabulary videos, how-to videos and interviews.

OR EVEN: They could produce advertisements or commercials, public service announcements, or virtual field trips using MinecraftEDU.

AND FOR THE TEACHER: Have students publish their creations to Flipgrid or on their Seesaw Journal. Teachers can create class teasers videos to spark student interest in a subject before you begin a unit.

Upload an exemplar to your class Seesaw Journals or Classroom Team. You could also have students create tutorial videos and then publish them to Flipgrid. If you teach older students, have them promote this Grid and gain viewership by sharing it to social media. Your class could also have a Facebook page and class Twitter account that they share videos to as well.

TRIPS TO FOREIGN COUNTRIES—Foreign language students can put together a virtual trip to a famous city, then narrate the trip in the foreign language to help them practice conversational speech and authentic accents. This can be done using Adobe Spark Video.

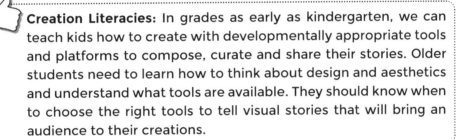

Creation Literacies: In grades as early as kindergarten, we can teach kids how to create with developmentally appropriate tools and platforms to compose, curate and share their stories. Older students need to learn how to think about design and aesthetics and understand what tools are available. They should know when to choose the right tools to tell visual stories that will bring an audience to their creations.

ADOBE SPARK VIDEO

ACCESS BY GOING TO: spark.adobe.com

WHAT IS ADOBE SPARK VIDEO? Adobe Spark Video is a web-based free video and audio creation platform. It can be accessed from any device with online access at spark.adobe.com. It is part of a creativity suite that also includes Adobe Post and Adobe Page.

GREAT BECAUSE students can easily create impressive slide presentations and **visual stories** to demonstrate their learning. Students can add their own images and edit up to thirty seconds of video on each slide. They can use their own original images or access the creative commons for high-quality free images that are available within the app. They can also choose from a variety of free music options to set the tone.

When students are provided with opportunities to demonstrate their learning using spark video they are being asked to think critically about a topic, make meaning, synthesize and design something that teaches others pushing their critical thinking in the topic they are learning about.

SET UP IS MODERATE. Once the school or district has access to Adobe's free EDU accounts, the student will have access to all the features of the tool on their own account. **infused.link/sparklogin**.

> **Note:** School accounts adhere to American federal privacy laws and are Ferpa and Coppa compliant. Students log in as a student using their school-issued account. Make sure this is set up first by having your school IT or leadership head over to **spark.adobe.com/edu**

STUDENTS TURN IN WORK BY uploading a shareable link to a curation tool like Padlet, Wakelet or Flipgrid, or they can share the link in their OneNote or Classroom Teams. **infused.link/sparkvideo**

ALLOWS STUDENTS TO tell **visual stories** that contain complexity, even though they are simple to use. They can also use a story template provided at the beginning of the projects and scaffold different story-telling elements to accomplish a number of objectives. They can promote an idea, explain an event, follow a hero's journey, create a "show and tell," narrate a personal growth story, and even teach a lesson.

WHAT'S GREAT IS THAT students can use Adobe Spark Video to learn foundational creation literacies.

Some visual story platforms allow a lot of unnecessary choices in colors and templates. With Spark, creative constraints are built-in with limited templates, teaching students to make smart aesthetic choices that lead to visually pleasing creations.

Check out Adobe's Edex community and find helpful tutorials and lessons at **edex.adobe.com**.

SHOWS YOU INFORMATION IN THIS WAY: In a horizontal-chronological timeline when spark video is unpublished and as a video once published.

There is a dashboard that allows you to edit your work later on if needed, as well as download it as an MP4.

IDEAS

- **Create student introduction videos!** Have students produce videos about themselves that they share on Flipgrid, so students can learn about each other.

- **Teach digital citizenship!** Create pledge videos detailing how students will appropriately use technology in their classrooms.

- **Document learning over time!** Take pictures of students' analog processes of work and have them produce a visual story inserting pictures and explaining their thinking process from the beginning to the end of their project.

- **Use for Social Media!** Students can curate and share Adobe Spark videos on your classroom social media account.

SWAY

ACCESS BY GOING TO: sway.com

WHAT IS SWAY? Sway is a resource that allows students to engage in digital storytelling using digital media that showcases their understanding of content in a meaningful, visual way.

GREAT BECAUSE students are able to visualize their learning and tell the story of the content in a way that makes sense to them by including text, images, video, audio files, and other media .

SET UP IS EASY. Students can access Sway through www.sway.com or by clicking the Sway tile located in their Microsoft portal located at office.com. Because Sway is web-based, it can be accessed from any device.

STUDENTS TURN IN WORK BY sharing the link to their Sway directly with their teacher. A Sway can also be embedded into another Sway or into OneNote, for example.

ALLOWS YOU TO start from scratch and personalize your presentation, select from one of hundreds of pre-populated templates, or import a Word document or PowerPoint slideshow directly into Sway. If students import a Word or PowerPoint into Sway, Sway will format what it thinks the presentation should look like. Students are then able to use this as a starting point and make adjustments as needed. For more information on creating a Sway, visit **infused.link/howtosway**.

WHAT'S GREAT IS THAT students can work independently, or easily collaborate on their digital storytelling projects, bringing the content to life.

SHOWS YOU THE INFORMATION IN THIS WAY: Play the presentation either vertically or horizontally, or by clicking the forward and backward arrows to manually advance to the next card of the Sway. Sways can also be looped and presented in autoplay.

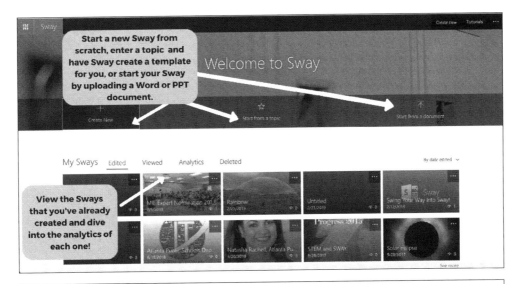

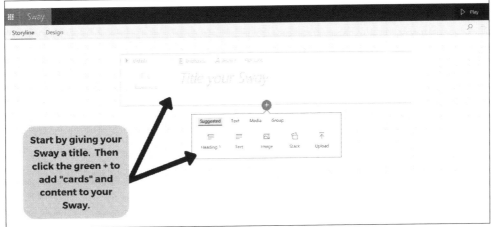

IDEAS

- **Demonstrate media literacy strategies!** Students can use Sway as a final place to showcase or document their writing assignments. Students will need to critically think about which images and organizational structures help bring that story or writing assignment to life.

- **Create a timeline of events!** Have students develop a timeline that shows a clear understanding of a storyline in history or science. They can use Sway to retell a historical event or even the story of a cool scientific discovery.

- **Share a summary!** Have students create a Sway that shows a summary of a story or idea they are reading about in class.

- **Promote cultural awareness!** Have students use Sway to promote Techquity, a term promoted by Ken Shelton, to help educators effectively use technology to create culturally responsive classrooms.

- **Tell important stories!** Have students research a person from their own race or ethnicity, use images and text to create biographical design projects to tell the story of someone important who might be excluded from a typical textbook.

- **Widen students' margins!** Encourage and support students in a culturally responsive learning experience by gathering information and resources from different points of view on the same event or experience, especially points of view from marginalized people and communities. Have that process documented and those stories told through a Sway project.

- **Make local connections!** Use Sway for representations of project-based learning that is aligned with students making real-life connections between the academic content and their own neighborhoods, cultures, and environments. Use the rich multimedia in Sway to better tell the story.

Demonstrations of Learning
THINK-PIC-SHARE

3

WHY WE DO THIS: We must teach our students how to illustrate their ideas in a digital world. After all, developing visual literacy is essential to becoming both digitally literate and fluent. In a "think-pic-share," students learn how to summarize and retell using graphics and images.

HOW USING "THINK-PIC-SHARE" MAKES THINKING VISIBLE: When implementing "think-pic-share" into your lessons, initially ask your students to think about and summarize what they've learned. Then have them find a picture that accurately represents the summary of their learning and add their thoughts in text to that graphic using Adobe Spark Post. Have them share their pic on something like Seesaw or Teams.

HOW USING "THINK-PIC-SHARE" AMPLIFIES STUDENT VOICE: When we ask our students to make a "think-pic-share," we're giving each of them a chance to create something using their own unique ideas. In making their creative choices, they demonstrate their own understanding of the concept.

HOW "THINK-PIC-SHARE" ALLOWS STUDENTS TO SHARE THEIR WORK: Having students publish their "think-pic-share" in a sharing space such as Seesaw or Teams allows them to consider an authentic audience and compare their ideas and perspectives with those of their peers.

What Students Can Create

YOU COULD TRY: Have your students write a six-word summary about what they just learned.

OR EVEN: Try doing a quick reflection with your students using Adobe Post so they can learn thinking strategies, such as the following one from *Making Thinking Visible* by Ron Ritchhart, Mark Church, and Karin Morrison.

FOR THE TEACHER: Get your students excited about an upcoming unit by sending them secret clues or a hook before a unit even begins. You could make your initial message through Adobe Post and then send to the students using Seesaw or Teams.

"The future belongs to a different kind of person with a different kind of mind: artists, inventors, storytellers—creative and holistic 'right-brain' thinkers."

— **Daniel Pink**

ADOBE SPARK POST

ACCESS BY GOING TO: spark.adobe.com

WHAT IS ADOBE SPARK POST Adobe Spark Post is a way for students to create visually appealing graphics. Students can amplify their voice using a visual graphic that uses images, icons, and words. Access it online from any device at **spark.adobe.com**.

Tanya Avrith

GREAT BECAUSE the app is easy to use and helps students with little graphic design knowledge create visually appealing graphics to communicate on a deeper level. This can take a valuable paper-and-pen artistic experience, make it digital, and allow students to share to a wider audience.

SETUP IS INTERMEDIATE. Once the school or district has access to the free Adobe EDU accounts, students can begin to create using all the features of the tool—including fonts, images, and stylistic settings.

Even if teachers are not familiar with digital graphics, adding them to the learning process enhances engagement. We have provided step-by-step instructions to help you get started.

ALLOWS STUDENTS TO work independently or with peers to create beautiful graphics that use symbolism to connect an image to a concept to enhance and clarify their learning.

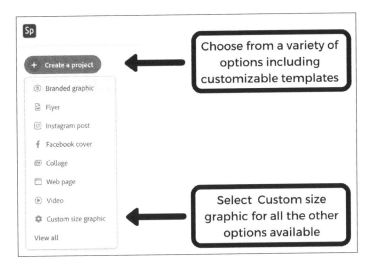

Note to Teachers: The school accounts adhere to American federal privacy laws and are FERPA and COPPA compliant. Students simply log in as a student, using their school-issued account. Make sure this is set up first by having your school IT or leadership head over to **spark.adobe.com/edu**.

See also **infused.link/sparklogin**

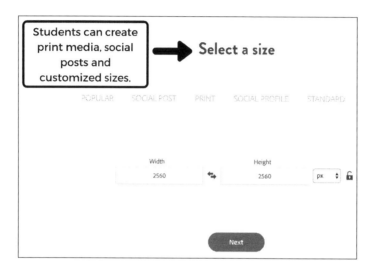

STUDENTS TURN IN WORK BY either inviting the teacher to the graphic or getting a link to copy and paste into other platforms such as Teams, Padlet, or Wakelet. You also can download the image as a file such as a PNG, JPEG, or PDF.

See: **infused.link/sparkshare**

WHAT'S GREAT IS THAT so many high-quality images are available with this application! Students can easily learn to enhance their text-based projects with meaningful graphics.

SHOWS YOU THE INFORMATION as a rich visual. Adobe Spark Post allows you to come back and edit your work or download to print and share.

IDEAS
Visible Thinking Routines

- Have students use visible thinking routines to explain their thoughts and understanding and to better gauge where they are in the learning process. For more information, check out this resource from Harvard's Project Zero on Visible Thinking Routines: **infused.link/projectzero**.

- A few visible thinking routines to try with your students could also include these favorite reflection activities. Have students create them and then enhance them with graphics.

- **Headlines**—Students create a headline to summarize a concept or idea.
- **I Used to Think, Now I Think**—Students reflect on how their thinking has changed over the course of a lesson.
- **Six Word Summary**—Students summarize an idea or concept using only six words using Adobe Spark Post.

POWERPOINT

ACCESS BY GOING TO: powerpoint.office.com

WHAT IS PowerPoint? PowerPoint for Office 365 is a Microsoft presentation tool that allows students to easily collaborate, create slides, and present content and ideas in a visually appealing way. Available online and in a stand-alone app, PowerPoint makes it easy for students to demonstrate their learning, illustrate their ideas, and make their thinking visible.

GREAT BECAUSE it's easy to use. Following easy-to-understand directions, students can collaborate with multiple peers to create Think-Pic-Share slides that make their thinking visible. Creating clear and professional-looking slides enables students to demonstrate learning in a more accessible way. PowerPoint also integrates with many Microsoft tools and apps to help students create a more engaging presentation and share their thinking with a larger audience.

SETUP IS EASY. All that's needed is an Office 365 school account, which is available for free for teachers and students. To get started with a presentation, simply add an image to represent your thoughts or ideas, then add text for emphasis. You also could use the screen recording feature to have the student explain in their own words their thinking, images, and text choices.

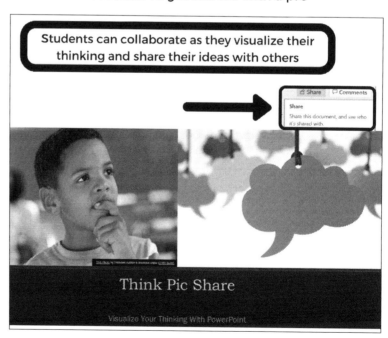

STUDENTS TURN IN WORK BY using the "share" feature in Power-Point. Students can control whether the person with whom they share their work has view-only or editing rights. They can send a link to their PowerPoint via email, or add the person's name directly to the project, and an automated notification will be sent to that person. Students also can turn in their PowerPoint through Microsoft Teams or by inserting their PowerPoint into OneNote Class Notebook.

ALLOWS STUDENTS TO collaboratively create beautiful presentations through the use of the designer feature. Students can easily add a variety of images as well as text to illustrate their thinking about a topic and to make their understanding visible. Many special effects features such as 3-D images and digital inking help students demonstrate their learning in creative and authentic ways.

WHAT'S GREAT IS THAT PowerPoint can be viewed and edited on multiple devices and platforms, making it easier for students to collaborate, both at school and at home. Students also have access to revision history to keep track of their thinking over time. PowerPoint also allows multiple students to have choice in creating amazing Think-Pic-Share slides or infographics to demonstrate their learning in ways that best suit their learning style.

GIVES YOU THE INFORMATION as a slideshow presentation, slideshow video, or a video that can be uploaded to Microsoft Stream, embedded in OneNote, or added to Microsoft Teams. PowerPoint lets students demonstrate their learning and make their thinking visible using a variety of rich media such as graphics, digital inking, 3-D images, pictures, and much more.

IDEAS

- See how creatively students can produce a visual demonstration of learning without text.
- Compose a social media post with an image and text to represent a historical figure and the facts that built their reputation.
- At the beginning of the school year, students can create a class ALL ABOUT ME, with an image and text to represent each student, to enable students to get to know their classmates.

Demonstrations of Learning
SCREENCASTING

WHY WE DO THIS: Screencasting helps students capture, explain, and reflect on the work that is on their screen.

HOW SCREENCASTING MAKES THINKING VISIBLE: It allows students to add narrated explanations and reflections that better explain their learning process to a basic document or digital artifact, such as a poster. To do this, students simply show the artifact on the screen and record their thinking. You could then use these recordings to see whether your students demonstrate their understanding of the learning targets.

HOW SCREENCASTING AMPLIFIES STUDENT VOICE: It gives all students a chance to explain their understanding and thinking, using a tool other than the written word.

HOW SCREENCASTING ALLOWS STUDENTS TO SHARE THEIR WORK: Screencasting gives your students the opportunity to provide you and their parents with a more in-depth understanding of where they are in their learning process, as well as to receive feedback from others.

WHAT STUDENTS CAN CREATE: Video reflective journals, explanations of their writing, Flipgrid videos, a story arc, and talk-through (place a story arc on screen, then talk through ideas for its plot and character development before starting the writing process), and narrated demonstrations of mathematical problem solving. This can be done using Flipgrid or Seesaw.

YOU COULD TRY: Have students hone their accents and conversational skills in a foreign language by reading and speaking in that language, adding narration to their PowerPoint, and presenting it to you alone, instead of the entire class.

OR EVEN: Let students make tutorials and dedicate an entire Grid on Flipgrid to your class's tutorials.

AND FOR THE TEACHER: Clone yourself! Leave directions for your students by creating differentiated tutorial videos for when you're home sick or at a conference.

POWERPOINT

ACCESS FROM ANY DEVICE: powerpoint.office.com

WHAT IS POWERPOINT? PowerPoint for Office 365 is Microsoft's Presentation Tool that allows students to demonstrate their learning and make their thinking visible by using the screen recording feature to record, explain, and reflect on what they have learned.

GREAT BECAUSE it allows students to record all activity and audio on the screen and demonstrate their learning in a variety of ways through individual and collaborative projects. Students can capture their thinking with screen recording and explain and reflect on the work they have completed.

SETUP IS EASY. All that's needed is an Office 365 school account that is available for free for teachers and students. Students can access PowerPoint from any device at **powerpoint.office.com**. To get started with screencasting in PowerPoint, click the **Insert** tab, select **media,** then select **screen recording.**

Students click "select area" and use the *+ crossbow* to capture the portion of the screen they want to record, then select "record." A countdown will appear on the screen before video and audio recording begins.

STUDENTS TURN IN WORK BY sharing their PowerPoint with the embedded screencast, using the share link provided, or by adding the teacher as a collaborator. Students also can turn in their work through Microsoft Teams, OneNote Class Notebook, or Microsoft Stream if they save it as a video.

ALLOWS STUDENTS TO capture any content and audio on their screen and share their thinking about the content in the form of reflective narratives or explanations. If screen recording is used via the Recorder tab in the Desktop app, in addition to recording the screen and audio, students also can record a video of themselves explaining their thinking and reflecting on their learning.

PRO TIP: A PowerPoint desktop app is available with an Office 365 subscription and offers another option for screen recording through the Recording tab. Setup for screen recording via the Recording tab is moderate for the initial setup, but each subsequent setup is easy.

WHAT'S GREAT IS THAT it allows students to demonstrate their learning via a digital platform, moving away from paper and pencil. It's a great way to capture student thinking regarding a specific learning target, gives teachers a way to clear up any misconceptions or misunderstandings, and provides a frame of reference for reteaching and differentiating instruction. PowerPoint's integration with other Microsoft products makes it a great tool to amplify student voice.

GIVES YOU THE INFORMATION in MP4 video format. Using the screen recorder in PowerPoint, the video automatically embeds into the PowerPoint slide the student creates and plays automatically when the slide is presented.

IDEAS

- With a short story prompt on their computer screen, students can record their thinking as they use their inference skills to create an ending to a story.

- Use the screen recorder to narrate and explain the steps students followed to solve a math equation.

- The screen recorder can be used to explain bias in research and demonstrate how different websites present the same content.

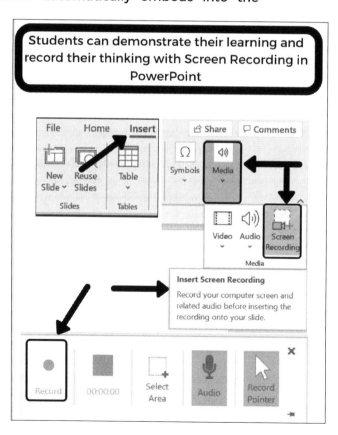

Students can demonstrate their learning and record their thinking with Screen Recording in PowerPoint

SCREENCAST-O-MATIC

WHAT IS SCREENCAST-O-MATIC/MICROSOFT TEAMS? Screencast-O-Matic is a free screen recording tool that integrates with Microsoft Teams and allows students to capture any area of their computer screen and provide both video and audio narration as they demonstrate or reflect on their learning.

GREAT BECAUSE students can record a variety of content, including narration that allows them to explain what they have learned. Screencast-O-Matic now integrates seamlessly with Microsoft Teams, making it easier for students to quickly share their learning and thinking with others.

SETUP IS MODERATE. To get started using Screencast-O-Matic, students will need to:

- Create a free account using your Office 365 school account at **screencast-o-matic.com**.
- Click on the "start recording for free" button, which takes them to "launch screen recorder."
- Once the recorder is launched, it will be downloaded.
- Students are prompted with a three-second countdown before recording begins.
- Students are given the option to record the screen, webcam, or both simultaneously, which allows students to have an inset video of them narrating the content on the screen.

STUDENTS TURN IN WORK BY saving the screen-recording as an MP4 file. Students also can turn in their work by saving their work to Screencast-O-Matic, which gives students the option to use the "quick share" feature to share the video directly to Microsoft Teams. To share to Microsoft Teams, students must use their Microsoft Office 365 login to create their Screencast-O-Matic account.

ALLOWS STUDENTS TO record up to fifteen minutes of video with student-created narrations that allow them to demonstrate their understanding of the content. Students are also able to add music and upload a caption file using the free version of Screencast-O-Matic, which allows them to make their video-based demonstrations of learning even more dynamic.

WHAT'S GREAT IS THAT it allows students to share their screen recordings to a variety of external platforms, such as Microsoft Teams, Twitter, or Facebook. When students are creating content for an authentic purpose or an external audience, the final product is typically created at a higher quality level.

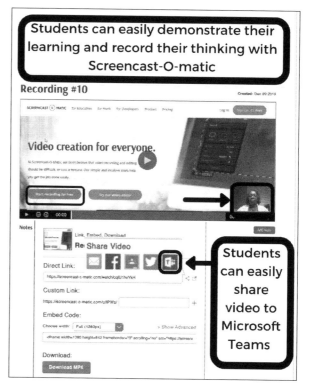

GIVES YOU THE INFORMATION IN THIS WAY: Once the recorder launches, a dotted line of the area that is being recorded appears. Screencast-O-Matic also shows students how their onscreen video will appear as they begin to capture their screen. Screencast-O-Matic shows the content that students record in MP4 video format.

IDEAS

- Record the presentation of a book report students create, using Microsoft Sway, PowerPoint, or Buncee.

- Create a how-to video tutorial explaining how to simplify fractions.

- Record a travel video sharing information about culture, customs, and people for a Geography unit.

- Have students record a screencast explaining their writing process and what they are trying to prove or explain. This way the teacher can better understand what the piece is supposed to communicate and match that up with the end product. The student can also explain the process from start to finish so the teacher can better understand the process.

Demonstrations of Learning
COLLABORATIVE STUDENT CREATIONS
WITH SLIDES

WHY WE DO THIS: Collaborative tools give students the opportunity to work on a platform that is easy to use, edit, and share with others. They can do this collaboratively, in a group, or in partners.

HOW COLLABORATIVE STUDENT CREATIONS MAKE THINKING VISIBLE: These projects provide students an opportunity to show and reflect on their learning while working with and receiving feedback from their peers.

HOW COLLABORATIVE STUDENT CREATIONS AMPLIFY STUDENT VOICE: They give each student a space in which to develop and share their ideas. Students can then add to their peers' work, amplifying the class's overall learning.

HOW COLLABORATIVE STUDENT CREATIONS ALLOW STUDENTS TO SHARE THEIR WORK: Students can share their creations with each other and work on the overall product together. When they are done, they can publish their creations to the web and share with others, providing opportunities to receive valuable feedback on their creations from their peers or from outside experts.

WHAT STUDENTS CAN CREATE: Of course, they can make collaborative presentations, but let's go further than that and be more creative.

YOU COULD TRY

> **SIX-WORD SUMMARIES**—Students do a six-word summary of an event or a chapter, then share it with the class using PowerPoint, Buncee, Adobe Spark Post, or Seesaw.

> **100-WORD CHALLENGE**—Students collaborate on the weekly writing prompt using a shared PowerPoint presentation. Each student works on their own slide and then takes it into Flipgrid or Seesaw to read it aloud.

TIP: To teach digital literacy, point students toward social media so they can gather an even more dynamic audience and gain responses and perspectives from around the globe.

USE TEMPLATES—Using a creative template such as a fake Instagram feed, have students create profiles for characters from the lesson, or even personifications of science and math concepts.

OR EVEN

CREATION GALLERIES—Use PowerPoint to create a digital gallery of work that showcases individual student creations, or share collaboratively in one slide deck.

AND FOR THE TEACHER: Explain your directions and learning targets in PowerPoint, then record using the screen recording option.

"When ideas and related concepts can be encapsulated in an image, the brain remembers the information associated with that image."

– Katrina Schwartz

BUNCEE

ACCESS BY GOING TO: buncee.com

@TheMerrillsEDU

WHAT IS BUNCEE? Buncee is a web-based tool for creating interactive multimedia presentations.

GREAT BECAUSE it gives students a space to collaborate and work together and offers multiple ways to help students visualize, voice, and communicate their learning while helping to develop and strengthen skills such as creativity and collaboration. You can share a Buncee assignment in Teams—this video tutorial shows you how: **infused.link/bunceeteams**.

SETUP IS EASY. Teachers can log in with an educator-created username or Microsoft account. They can form classes and create student accounts. Primary educators also have the option of enabling "one password for all," a feature that uses the same password for all students.

STUDENTS TURN IN WORK BY Students can create a Buncee together, and when finished they have the ability to share their work directly with the teacher or by sharing a unique link generated automatically. This link can then be shared through other platforms such as Seesaw, Flipgrid, Microsoft Teams, and OneNote.

ALLOWS YOU TO integrate content from both external and internal sources as well as create content directly on each slide. A toolbar provides ease of accessibility and preview without students ever navigating away from the slide. Students can easily collaborate with each other within the presentation.

WHAT'S GREAT IS THAT Buncee allows students to move beyond simply adding text and photos. Students can include animations, backgrounds, and audio recordings, and they can even have Microsoft Immersive Reader embedded into their creation. It also now integrates into Flipgrid, OneNote, Teams, and Wakelet. This means you can insert a Buncee presentation directly into these platforms with a click of a button.

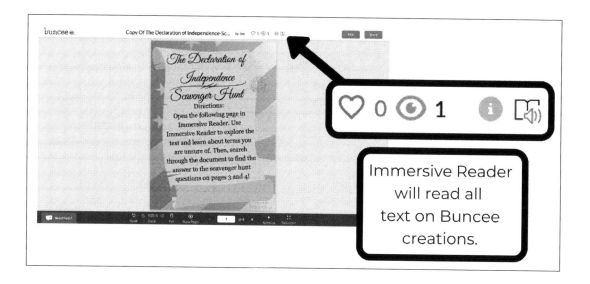

Immersive Reader will read all text on Buncee creations.

SHOWS YOU INFORMATION IN THIS WAY: Students begin with a blank slide called the "creation window." All activity happens within this space. The toolbar at the right controls all incoming multimedia content, which can be from one's own library, the internet, or the preexisting Buncee collection.

IDEAS

- Students can collaborate and create a class yearbook for the end of the year, showcasing all the learning from the year.
- Students can work together to develop an interactive dictionary of words with various animations, stickers, and design to show the meanings of grade-level words.
- Watch the Buncee Tutorial Playlist at **infused.link/bunceeplaylist**

POWERPOINT

ACCESS FROM ANY DEVICE: powerpoint.office.com

WHAT IS POWERPOINT? PowerPoint for Office 365 is widely known as a presentation tool that allows students to easily collaborate, create slides, and present content and ideas in a visually appealing way. PowerPoint, however, is so much more than that; it allows students to creatively demonstrate their learning and share their thinking with a wider audience beyond the classroom.

GREAT BECAUSE PowerPoint is great because of its ease of use. It allows students to demonstrate their learning while also working collaboratively with their peers to create slides using a variety of media such as drawings, 3-D images, video, audio, and ink to math or ink to shapes.

SETUP IS EASY. All that's needed is an Office 365 school account. To get started collaborating with others in PowerPoint, log in with your Office 365 account select **share**, and begin to collaborate by sending someone the link or adding their name. To collaborate in the PowerPoint App, you will need to save the presentation to OneDrive first and then follow the steps for sharing.

Multiple students can easily collaborate and demonstrate their learning with PowerPoint

STUDENTS TURN IN WORK BY using the share feature in PowerPoint. With this option, students can control whether the person whom they share their work has view-only or editing rights. Students can also turn in their PowerPoint through Microsoft Teams or by inserting their PowerPoint into a OneNote Class Notebook.

ALLOWS STUDENTS TO collaboratively create beautiful presentations using a variety of media that makes it easy for them to demonstrate their understanding and make their thinking visible by using screencasting and the digital inking feature to record their understanding of solving specific math equations or creating an infographic or political poster to demonstrate their understanding of propaganda.

WHAT'S GREAT IS THAT PowerPoint online automatically saves in the PowerPoint app after it has been saved to OneDrive initially. Students also have access to revision history to keep track of their thinking over time or go back to other editions of their work.

GIVES YOU THE INFORMATION as a slideshow presentation, slideshow video, or a video that can be uploaded to Microsoft Stream or embedded in OneNote or added to Microsoft Teams. PowerPoint lets students demonstrate their learning and make their thinking visible by using a variety of rich media such as graphics, digital inking, 3-D images, Forms, and much more. They also can use the Screen Record feature to explain and expound on their ideas and process.

IDEAS

PowerPoint can be used collaboratively by students to do the following:

- Create a how-to demonstration video
- Create a visual representation/presentation without text
- Create a social media historical biography via PowerPoint

Demonstrations of Learning
COLLABORATIVE STUDENT WRITING

6

WHY WE DO THIS: Collaborative writing allows students to work together to expand on their ideas and amplify the writing process.

HOW COLLABORATIVE WRITING MAKES THINKING VISIBLE: When students work together, they must be able to explain their thoughts and ideas to each other. Microsoft Word, Microsoft Teams, OneNote Class Notebook, Book Creator, and Adobe Spark Page all allow for this critical strategy.

HOW COLLABORATIVE WRITING AMPLIFIES STUDENT VOICE: Even students who are slow to write can often produce more written material when they are working in pairs. Collaboration allows students to brainstorm together and bounce ideas off their peers for input, taking advantage of someone else's perspective in a less stressful setting. To reduce the pressure individual students feel to compose a writing assignment individually, consider allowing at least half of student papers to be co-written.

HOW COLLABORATIVE WRITING ALLOWS STUDENTS TO SHARE THEIR WORK: Students begin by sharing first with their collaboration partner and later, if they choose, with a larger audience. You can consider using Adobe Pages as a final draft and place for the work to be shared.

WHAT STUDENTS CAN CREATE: Your students can make documents, drawings, tables, journals, and reading PDFs. They can even produce a class newspaper or magazine.

YOU COULD TRY: Have students do a collaborative writing assignment with at least two classmates. Here they can jump into the same document and learn how to work together toward a common goal.

AND FOR THE TEACHER: Using the collaborative environment of OneNote to create a HyperDoc student-facing digital lesson.

ONENOTE

ACCESS BY GOING TO: onenote.office.com

WHAT IS ONENOTE? OneNote is a digital notebook that automatically saves and syncs your notes as you work. You can type information directly into your notebook or copy and paste it from other apps and web pages. It's a great tool for students to collaborate with peers as they demonstrate their learning.

@apsitnatasha

GREAT BECAUSE as students collaborate and work together within One-Note, they pay closer attention to what they write because they are sharing it with their peers. OneNote makes it easier to make thinking visible. Students can show their work in OneNote and voice record their thoughts as they talk about learning and further explain their ideas.

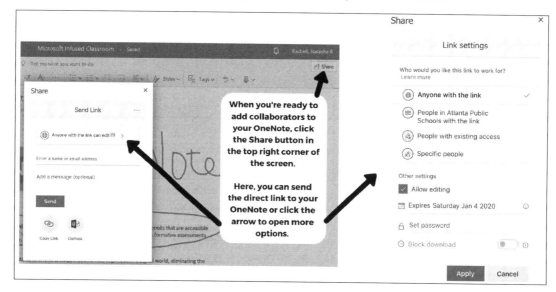

SETUP IS EASY. Users need an Office 365 school account, which is free for teachers and students. Students and teachers can create digital notebooks and organize them via sections and pages to meet their needs.

STUDENTS TURN IN WORK BY publishing it directly inside their OneNote notebooks. Because OneNote automatically saves in real time, there is no need to worry about each collaborator saving their portion of the notebook as they work.

If there are included links to other tools to assess students such as Pear Deck, Flipgrid, or Microsoft Forms, teachers would access those data within those tools. For example, if teachers provided a quiz via Forms within OneNote to formatively assess groups of students, those results would be accessed within Forms and not OneNote.

ALLOWS YOU TO give students the freedom to demonstrate their learning in the manner that works for them. They can work in real time with other students. They can type, draw, audio record, and include images and videos to show their understanding of the content. Collaborating in OneNote works for all students because each student can personalize their experience for clarity and understanding.

WHAT'S GREAT IS THAT incorporating Learning Tools and Immersive Reader into this experience further levels the playing field and ensures that all students have the tools they need to be successful. Even though a group of students may be collaborating and working within the same OneNote notebook, each of them can access the learning tools on their individual devices to personalize the learning experience for themselves.

SHOWS YOU THE INFORMATION in an online notebook or in the OneNote app. When students are collaborating within the same OneNote, they (along with their teacher) can see which students have added to or made changes within the notebook by viewing the initials of each author next to their changes. To enable this feature, click "View" and then "Show Authors."

WORD

WHAT IS WORD? Microsoft Word is a word processing application that provides an opportunity for both individual and collaborative writing.

GREAT BECAUSE Word documents live in the Office 365 Cloud and can be accessed from any device. These documents can be shared with anyone, anywhere in the world, at any time, allowing for collaboration from multiple locations at any time.

SETUP IS EASY. Word is free for teachers and students. Students can log in to Word through the Microsoft Portal at **office.com,** using their Office 365 account.

STUDENTS TURN IN WORK BY sharing the link to their Microsoft Word document directly with their teacher, or by making the teacher a collaborator on their document. Students also can share the link to their Word document in OneNote, Flipgrid, Teams, or Sway.

ALLOWS YOU TO collaborate easily from any device. Multiple students can work together on the same document and view, edit, or comment at the same time. Learn more about how your students can use Microsoft Word for real-time collaboration: **infused.link/collaborateword.**

WHAT'S GREAT IS THAT creating Microsoft Word documents within Office 365 automatically saves the content as students are working. Students are able to work collaboratively on Word documents, and because content automatically saves, students working together can view changes and updates to the document in real time.

By clicking "View" and then "Immersive Reader," students can personalize their learning experience, even in a collaborative document. Because students are working on their own individual devices, using Immersive Reader will only personalize their own experience and not affect other students working within the same document.

Students also can use the "Add-ins" feature to personalize their Word experience even more.

SHOWS YOU THE INFORMATION in text format, and images and graphics can easily be incorporated.

IDEAS

- Use the "Dictate" button for talk-to-text ideas. Once students click the "Dictate" button and give their device permission to access the microphone, students can dictate from a selection of multiple languages.

- Use the "Ideas" button to refine writing. This helps to align a common voice and language throughout the document as collaboration occurs. As students are typing, "Ideas" will make suggestions to improve student writing based on clarity, conciseness, formality, inclusiveness, punctuation conventions, sensitive geographical references, and vocabulary.

- Create resumes for fictional characters in books and stories in the Resume template.

- Plan a fictional trip and collaborate to examine location, weather, food, economic costs, and other important elements.

Demonstrations of Learning
WHITEBOARDS

WHY WE DO THIS: Whiteboards help students capture, explain, and reflect on their learning, using a more powerful platform that allows for animation, compare and contrast, math problems, and sketchnoting. Basically anything your students need to do can be done on a whiteboard, the best ones being Seesaw, Microsoft Whiteboard, Flipgrid, and OneNote.

HOW COLLABORATIVE INTERACTIVE WHITEBOARDS MAKES THINKING VISIBLE: It allows students to demonstrate their understanding and their thinking process. Students are able to show their work on the screen while recording themselves telling us what they are thinking, what steps they took, and their thought process behind the work.

HOW COLLABORATIVE INTERACTIVE WHITEBOARDS AMPLIFY STUDENT VOICE: It gives them a place to express their learning in their own creative way, with a more powerful set of tools and functions. With these enhanced features, their ability to share what they have learned is amplified.

HOW COLLABORATIVE INTERACTIVE WHITEBOARDS ALLOW STUDENTS TO SHARE THEIR WORK: Students can publish their creations to share with the class or with a global audience. They can even share with another student and work on the creation together.

WHAT STUDENTS CAN CREATE:

TUTORIALS—Students can create tutorials of math, a foreign language, or any concept taught in class. They can then use the videos to teach one another or curate a help channel for students in younger grades. The best videos also can be used to help differentiate instruction for other students in the class. These can be created in Flipgrid and Seesaw or even Adobe Spark Video, which is not specifically discussed in this section. The Microsoft Photos App can be considered for video creation as well.

COMPARE AND CONTRAST VIDEO—Have students curate two different videos of a similar event, such as a time lapse of a science experiment. Then capture their understanding of why they turned out differently using the record feature, with reflections and real scientific reasoning.

SKETCHNOTING WITH VOICEOVERS—This is great for visual learners. Students sketch out their notes and ideas using mind mapping or sketchnoting techniques, then narrate that thinking process using the record feature. This can be done in OneNote and then reflected on using the audio recording feature or taken into Flipgrid or Seesaw for ease in sharing with the entire class.

INTERACTIVE TIMELINES—Have students use PowerPoint to place historical events in chronological order using text and images, then recording their voice and explanations using the record feature and insert into Microsoft Whiteboard.

OR EVEN:

BLACKOUT POETRY: Have students take a picture of a poem or story and use the marker pens in SeeSaw or Flipgrid to black all the words except the ones they want to use to create their own blacked-out piece of poetry.

Check out this blog post as an example:
HollyClark.org/blackoutpoetry.

LETTER AND LETTER SOUNDS TREASURE HUNT—Students must explore their class and school to look for examples of beginning letter sounds or images of objects that begin with that letter. Students then create a screencast of the treasure hunt, explaining their discoveries. This can be done using OneNote or Seesaw.

ONENOTE

ACCESS BY GOING TO: onenote.office.com

WHAT IS ONENOTE? OneNote is an infinite canvas notebook application that can also be used as a collaborative online whiteboard. It can be used to allow students to digitally show and create content, import different file formats, and audio record as they demonstrate their learning.

GREAT BECAUSE students are able to collaborate, create, and reflect on their learning. OneNote allows students to type text, create audio files, and sketchnote their learning, organizing it in a way that makes sense for them.

SETUP IS EASY. Users must have an Office 365 school account, which is free for teachers and students. Students and teachers can create digital notebooks and organize them via sections and pages—with one of the pages being used as a whiteboard.

STUDENTS TURN IN WORK BY publishing it directly inside their OneNote notebooks. Because OneNote automatically saves in real time, there is no need to worry about each collaborator saving their portion of the OneNote notebook that they are working on in the whiteboard to show their learning.

ALLOWS YOU TO visualize thinking and demonstrate learning. OneNote also allows students to collaborate with one another to learn and grow from meaningful feedback, building self-esteem and self-confidence as they illustrate their thought process. When needed, students can create tutorials for content review. Another awesome feature of OneNote is the digital drawing feature, which allows for sketchnoting. Students can use the audio feature in conjunction with digital drawing to explain the thinking behind their creation.

For more on sketchnoting, visit this Wakelet collection:
infused.link/sketchnoting.

WHAT'S GREAT IS THAT using OneNote as a whiteboard allows students to personalize their learning and notetaking and organize it in a way that makes sense to them. They can annotate over text to really digest the content. Students also can create mind maps and different graphic organizers to organize their learning. In addition, students have a choice between text-based, written (sketchnotes), and audio-recorded notes. In math, students can record and work out problems and play them back step-by-step as they progress through content.

SHOWS YOU THE INFORMATION on a digital notebook from any device. Teachers see their students' Class Notebooks at any time to assess progress. When students are collaborating within the same OneNote, they (along with their teacher) can see which students have added to or made changes within the notebook by viewing the initials of each author next to their changes. To enable this feature, click "View" and then "Show Authors."

IDEAS

- For a step up from flash cards, use the digital drawing feature to write out their sight words. They can then incorporate the audio recording feature to pronounce and spell the words as well.

- Students can screen capture important websites or images from the web that are needed for research. They can then bring them into the OneNote notebook and annotate over them to emphasize meaningful information.

- Bring math equations to life with the Math Tools. Students can type or digital ink their math equations, and OneNote will create an interactive graph that can be manipulated and then inserted onto the OneNote page for a multifaceted representation of a problem.

- Don't forget to press "record" and have students add their thinking behind solving the math equation with the audio tool.

MICROSOFT WHITEBOARD

ACCESS BY GOING TO: whiteboard.office.com

WHAT IS MICROSOFT WHITEBOARD? Microsoft Whiteboard is Microsoft's stand-alone infinite canvas that allows students to work collaboratively and combine both their ideas and content to demonstrate their learning and make their thinking visible. Whiteboard is available both online at **whiteboard.microsoft.com** and as an app that can be downloaded from the Microsoft Store or the IOS store.

GREAT BECAUSE it is very robust and has a variety of content that can be inserted onto the Whiteboard canvas that allows students to demonstrate what they have learned in a unique way.

Students organize and share their thoughts and ideas, add a variety of content such as PowerPoint or Word documents that they have created, and add camera pics or images, text, notes, lists, or Edge searches to demonstrate their learning and make their thinking visible. Students also can invite their peers to collaborate while working in Whiteboard.

SETUP IS EASY, and it's available to download for free at the Microsoft Store or in the IOS store. To create a new Whiteboard, simply click on the + or click on a previous Whiteboard to continue working. You will need your Office 365 login to begin using Microsoft Whiteboard.

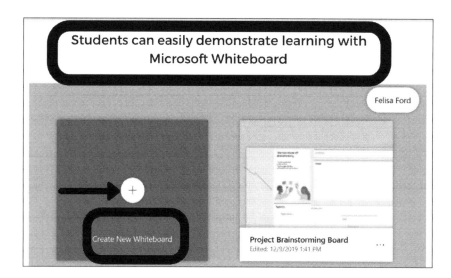

STUDENTS TURN IN WORK BY exporting their Whiteboard as a PNG file and sharing that file. Students also can click on the ellipsis in the upper right corner to post the Whiteboard to Microsoft Teams.

ALLOWS STUDENTS TO demonstrate their learning and understanding of a concept while making what they have learned visible. Students can invite collaborators to work together. Students can customize or change the background and add a variety of content, choosing images, text, post-it notes, or pictures, and they can add previously created content such as PowerPoints or Word documents.

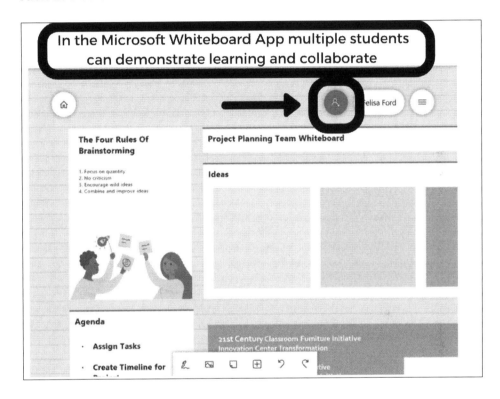

WHAT'S GREAT IS THAT it allows individual students and student groups to seamlessly demonstrate their learning and make their thinking visible. They can add outside content and research through Bing to further illustrate their understanding. Additionally, Microsoft Whiteboard can easily be used to curate content—even if it's previously created—in one platform. Students also can add a more personal touch and customize their Whiteboard. One of the best features is that it saves automatically and it integrates with Microsoft Teams, so students don't have to worry about losing work.

GIVES YOU THE INFORMATION on an infinite canvas. Students have the freedom to lay out their content based on their preference. Whiteboard also has a dashboard as the home landing page that shows all the Whiteboards the students have created, the name of the Whiteboard, and the last time the Whiteboard was edited.

 ## IDEAS

- Create a collaborative end-of-unit whiteboard in which students can contribute one thing they learned from the unit, using any media available in Whiteboard. Teachers can then project the Whiteboard as a gallery for parents to see when they visit the classroom.

- Create a graphic organizer comparing two historical figures or literary works.

- Students can create a Whiteboard documenting the process they followed to complete a science lab.

- Students can use Whiteboard to debate a topic by providing the pros and cons of an argument, with supporting details, using a variety of content.

MICROSOFT
LEARNING WITH TEAMS

WHAT IS MICROSOFT TEAMS? Microsoft Teams is the Office 365 all-encompassing platform that serves as a digital hub for classrooms by promoting communication, collaboration, conversations, and assignments, as well as creating and curating content. It is the perfect platform to showcase evidence of student learning and thinking. Think of it as the classroom communication hub.

GREAT BECAUSE It is organized into channels. You can add a different channel for every topic. It enables the seamless integration of all Microsoft apps, including partner apps and external web pages, all within the Teams platform. With Microsoft Teams, students have many options to demonstrate learning, from using Flipgrid shorts to creating a Buncee News Report to screen recording in PowerPoint, and collaborating seamlessly with peers. This ease of use and seamless integration with other educational tools allows students to focus on their thinking, demonstrate their learning, and make their thinking visible in a more engaging and authentic manner all in one place. To learn more about Microsoft Teams and other Office 365 apps, visit the Microsoft Education Help Center: **infused.link/mshelpcenter.**

SETUP IS EASY. Microsoft Teams is available in Office 365, IOS, and Android. Users must have an Office 365 school account, which is free for teachers and students. To get started, click on the Teams icon in Office 365 (**teams.microsoft.com**) or download the Teams App from the app store. Click on the + button to create a new team or join a team with a code.

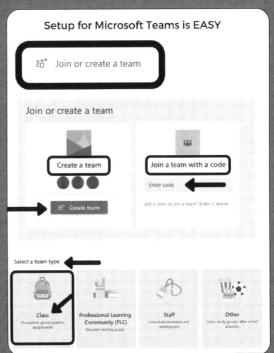

STUDENTS TURN IN WORK BY selecting a specific assignment card, or by navigating to the general channel for their class and select assignments. All upcoming assignments will appear in order of their due date. Students simply select the correct assignment card to open, view the details of the assignment, and follow the instructions to upload their work.

ALLOWS STUDENTS TO communicate, collaborate, curate, create, and demonstrate their learning without ever leaving the Teams hub. Students are able to work collaboratively on projects, work individually, or work in small groups. Microsoft Teams also allows students to create new documents from the Office apps (Word, Excel, PowerPoint, and OneNote) within Teams, upload documents from their computer, or add connectors with some popular apps such as Kahoot, Flipgrid, Wakelet, Buncee, YouTube, and Pear Deck.

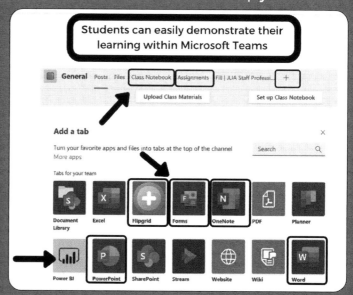

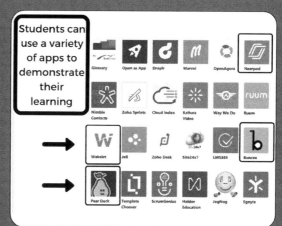

WHAT'S GREAT IS THAT Microsoft Teams is the all-encompassing digital hub that makes it easier for students to work more collaboratively and efficiently in the classroom. Teams helps support an inclusive classroom: with the Immersive Reader now available in Teams, all students can thrive regardless of ability. Microsoft Teams now has the Turnitin feature integrated to help promote authentic writing and creation of original content. Teachers also can collect a variety of student information on Teams at any time.

GIVES YOU THE INFORMATION by showing the name of the owner of the Team as well as the names of the Team members. Small group members are listed in different Team channels. A list of assignments is available, along with their due dates. Team members receive notifications for new assignments with available points and when their assignment has been graded.

IDEAS

- Use the channels feature of Teams to create small groups for primary students as they work together to improve phonemic awareness, comprehension, and automaticity.

- Working in Word in Teams, students can collaborate to create a comparative analysis of famous speeches, and then record themselves delivering their favorite speech in OneNote or PowerPoint.

- Have students visit the Microsoft Student Help Center for more ideas on how they can enhance creativity and wow their classmates at the same time: **infused.link/msstudenthelp**.

Formative Assessment

Tips for Differentiation

Demonstrations of Learning

Reflection and Curation

►Reflection and Curation
AND THE TOOLS TO USE

As educators, our job is to help students make meaning of concepts and ideas. We want them to construct knowledge and be creators of their learning, not just consumers that parrot information back to us. Ultimately, we want the experiences in our classroom to inspire curiosity and a love of learning that will last a lifetime.

Reflection is an essential practice for every learner-centered classroom. The truth is that this step of the learning process is often omitted, for the following reasons:

It is admittedly not an easy practice to master. And because students are so infrequently asked to reflect on their learning, they have trouble doing it well.

Many teachers have not themselves been taught to academically reflect, so they don't know where to begin teaching the process with their own students.

It takes time. Reflection is easy to skip when teachers are already rushing to cover content in their overcrowded curriculum.

We want to encourage you to be intentional about incorporating this valuable practice in your classroom.

We know this may be a new skill and that it will take some learning, but think of it as an educational adventure! When you see how much reflection helps your students understand the content, who they are as learners, and how they can apply their knowledge to future learning, you will be hooked. For us, it has been an adventure not unlike owning a puppy. You can't believe how much work it is, but when that puppy matures, it becomes your best friend.

As educators, we must teach students how to reflect. They need to understand that in all learning a specific time should be devoted to pausing, looking back at the journey, and considering how they arrived at true academic knowledge. This time of self-evaluation and reflection happens when students comment on, connect with, and reassess the learning process. This is assessment as learning, and it is often as important to student learning and growth as the content itself. A reflective classroom includes both oral and text-based reflections.

Reflection is grounded in questions and routines. You might have specific questions students learn to ask, or you might use a scaffolded approach that starts out easy and moves its way to much deeper internal reflections.

The end goal is to have students develop their own reflective practice.

After all, the skill of reflection is a transformational life skill. Imagine a world in which people critically reflected on the decisions they made and thoughtfully looked for ways they might do better next time. With that scenario in mind, which seems like a more important skill to teach students: reflection or the date of a battle in America's Civil War?

In this section, we will share a few technology tools that will allow for a rich, reflective process by students. These tools allow students to record their thinking, show their learning, and expound critically on the process.

Here are four easy ways for students to get started practicing the skill of reflection:

1) Keep a Journal or Diary

Using an app like Flipgrid or Seesaw, students can keep a written diary or video journal where they list three ways they learned that day or week. This helps students develop their vocabulary around how they learn and helps them uncover their learning preferences. This is done perfectly in a Flipgrid or Seesaw environment, or through OneNote.

For example, students might write or record the following prompts, giving details after each comment:

- I learned through prediction.
- I learned through context clues.
- I learned through talking with my neighbor.

For younger students, sentence stems might be a good place to start. For example, students might write or use the record feature in a Seesaw journal to explain the following thoughts:

- I was good at
- I liked
- I had problems with
- Next time I might

2) Write a Letter

Students can use SeeSaw or OneNote to write a short series of letters to themselves after each learning scenario. In the letter, they explain their learning process and the steps they took. They tell themselves how they could apply this learning in the real world.

3) Offer Some Advice

Using Flipgrid or SeeSaw, students could leave advice for themselves for their next unit. For example, they might offer recommendations on what they could do differently, discuss learning patterns, expound on strengths, and talk about how they might approach the next unit of study intentionally.

4) Create a Video Reflection

Students can use Screencast-O-Matic, Flipgrid, Seesaw, or even OneNote to record themselves explaining their learning and uncovering their thinking process using video reflections.

No matter where you begin or how you develop a rich and reflective program, it is a very important step in any learning scenario. More importantly, students should share their reflections with each other so they can build a bigger repertoire and toolkit of reflective practices. This should be an ongoing process that becomes more detailed over time.

FIRST, during the learning process and as you begin to wrap up a unit, decide how you'd like for your students to reflect, and then have them gather information on how they met their learning targets. You may begin the thought process by providing them with a scaffolded guiding question.

NEXT, choose a tool that will both assist students as they reflect on their learning journey and encourage the depth of thinking you're looking for. Go with an easy-to-use platform for the reflection piece. We shouldn't grade reflections, because grading them will only cause students to not be as critical or honest.

FINALLY, respond to your students' reflections so they know their ideas were heard, even though you didn't grade them. Use the data you gather from the students' work to further reflect on your own practices and adjust the unit.

TEACHERS: Now it is time for you to reflect on the unit. What went well? What fell flat? What would you carry into another unit? Teacher reflection is just as critical as student reflection for growth and understanding.

> "Alone we can do so little; together we can do so much."
>
> —Helen Keller

FLIPGRID

ACCESS BY GOING TO: flipgrid.com

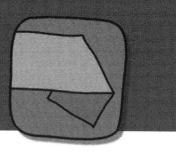

WHAT IS FLIPGRID? Flipgrid is a video-response platform featuring grids and topics. Think of it as a grid that helps flip your instruction. On a grid you can have topics that are unlimited and allow you to ask different discussion questions or prompts based on the overarching subject of the grid. Check out the free online FLIGRID course: **bit.ly/Flipgrid19**.

GREAT BECAUSE the grid environment empowers students to self-reflect as well as watch and respond to their classmates' videos. Even the students who are shy or slow to respond by raising their hands have a chance to participate with Flipgrid. It works great for students who just need a bit more time to process before they post. It also allows students to build articulate verbal reasoning skills as they post and respond. Video responses often prompt further discussions among students in the class.

SETUP IS EASY. You just name a grid, ask a question, and let the video responses begin. Each grid can have limitless topics. For example, name a grid "The Outsiders," and ask questions about the book as topics within that grid.

ALLOWS STUDENTS TO watch other student videos, self-reflect on their own learning, learn from each other, and compare their learning with that of their peers. This allows them to "think about thinking" and naturally produces a state of metacognition.

GIVES YOU THE INFORMATION IN THIS WAY: Fligprid lets your students create video responses on a grid that can be seen by those who have access to that grid. Great examples can be added to a mixtape to show the following period, or even the next year. You also can share a link with parents to that child's video if you would like.

WHAT IS GREAT IS THAT Flipgrid allows you to collaborate with other classrooms using the GridPals option at the top of the dashboard. It also has a fantastic Disco Library to help gather lesson ideas. Flipgrid teaches students the digital citizenship lessons of commenting and communicating effectively with others via video and media. (Note: Teachers need to spend a bit of time talking about proper commenting and meaningful replies first. Students spend their lives taking videos, taking selfies, and interacting on social media with a global audience, but they don't naturally know how to do this in a constructive way. Now teachers can harness the power and fun of social media in their classrooms.)

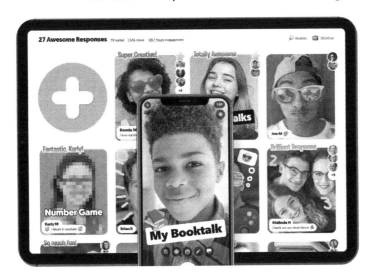

SHOWS YOU THE INFORMATION presented in an organized grid, which makes it highly visual, easy to navigate, and easy to access. From the student grid, the videos even play Netflix style, one after the other, making them easy to watch.

IDEAS

- **End of Unit Thinking Routine**—Use the powerful thinking routine "I used to think, now I think" to have students reflect on their learning at the end of the unit.
- **Math**—Students can explain their thinking about how they got to the solution of a math problem, using the Whiteboard or a visual.
- **Science**—Have students take time-lapse videos of science projects and upload those to a grid. They can use the comment feature to explain what happened during the process and briefly analyze the results.
- **Art**—Have students give their interpretations of an art piece. Then have them listen to the other student interpretations, reflecting on why they might be dramatically different or even the same.
- **English**—Have students explain their understanding after reading a chapter in a book.
- **Band**—Have a practice grid for each student where they can record themselves practicing and watch and reflect on their growth over time.

ONENOTE

ACCESS BY GOING TO: onenote.office.com

WHAT IS ONENOTE? OneNote is Microsoft's digital version of the tried and true three-ring binder that's been a staple in classrooms for years. OneNote is an infinite canvas digital notebook that promotes anytime, anywhere learning that can take place on any device, which makes it easier for students to curate content and reflect on their learning.

GREAT BECAUSE OneNote allows students to curate resources in one place and provides them the opportunity to reflect on their learning directly within the notebook. Students can create audio files within their notebook as they digest the content. They can make their thinking visible and demonstrate their learning by typing, adding audio, video, or images, or using digital ink on touch screen devices to show their understanding of the content. Students can work collaboratively as they curate new content and reflect on their learning.

SETUP IS EASY. Students can create digital notebooks and organize them via sections and pages to meet their needs. Users must have an Office 365 school account, which is free for teachers and students.

STUDENTS TURN IN WORK BY completing reflections within their individual Class Notebooks. Teachers are able to access the individual notebooks of each student for access to their thoughts and ideas, as they complete the reflection process.

ALLOWS YOU TO easily create a notebook and share it with teachers, parents, and peers for real-time access or collaboration. Students can access their OneNote notebooks on any device to continue creating or editing their content, organizing their ideas, thoughts, and notes. Students can customize pages by changing the background color or add notebook lined or graph paper to easily demonstrate learning for all subject areas.

Students can create sketchnotes, using the drawing tool to annotate and replay what they have drawn. Students can add images, video, audio, or research via websites, all without leaving OneNote. They can also embed or insert other Microsoft documents such as Word, PowerPoint, Sway, or Forms to create interactive content. OneNote allows students to reflect on the content they have created by recording, writing, or drawing their thoughts or ideas.

WHAT'S GREAT IS THAT students can author, create, and reflect on new and existing content, collaborate with peers, share their content, and complete any assignments all within their OneNote notebooks.

SHOWS YOU THE INFORMATION in a notebook layout with sections and pages that can be customized by name and color for each OneNote notebook that students create. This helps students organize their content, making it easier to search and find what they're looking for.

IDEAS

- Students can create portfolios, using OneNote to show and reflect the "best of the best" of their learning. Links to portfolios could be included in college applications or their resumes.

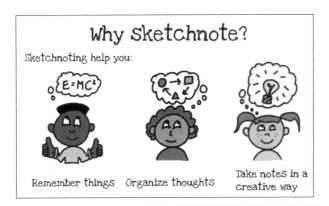

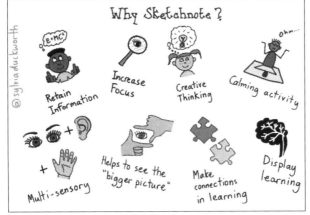

Images courtesy of @SylviaDucksworth

- Students can use the math assistant to support math practice and then use the recorder to reflect on their understanding. Students can also insert a Wakelet of their curated content into OneNote.

- Students can add an audio reflection tied to their sketchnotes or typed class notes.

- To learn more about having a day of sketchnoting in your school or classroom check out these resources at **infused.link/sketch**.

MICROSOFT TEAMS

ACCESS BY GOING TO: teams.office.com

WHAT IS MICROSOFT TEAMS? Microsoft Teams is an all-encompassing platform that serves as a digital hub for classrooms by promoting communication, collaboration, and conversations. Teams is a place where teachers can create and curate content. Teams is available online and as an app.

GREAT BECAUSE it is a one-stop shop that promotes seamless communication, collaboration, and content curation, as well as integration with other Microsoft apps and third-party apps, all within Teams—eliminating the need for students to open multiple webpages, tabs, and documents. With Microsoft Teams, students have many options to curate content and reflect on their learning while using a variety of apps, tools, and resources available in the Microsoft Teams platform. This ease of use allows students to seamlessly reflect on their learning and make their thinking visible in a more authentic manner.

SETUP IS EASY. Users only need an Office 365 school account. To get started, click on the Teams icon in Office 365 or go to **teams.office.com**. Students can also download the Teams App from the app store. Click on the + button to create a new team or join a team with a code. Follow the prompts to create or join your team and then channel.

STUDENTS TURN IN WORK BY using the turn in assignment button integrated into Teams. They can also turn in work by using the student section of the OneNote Class Notebook.

ALLOWS STUDENTS TO simultaneously reflect on the work that they have completed and curate content. Teams allows students to create new documents from the Office

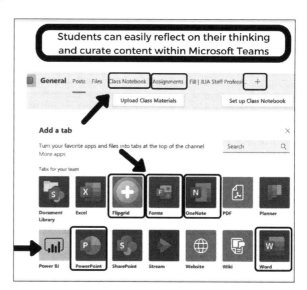

Students can easily reflect on their thinking and curate content within Microsoft Teams

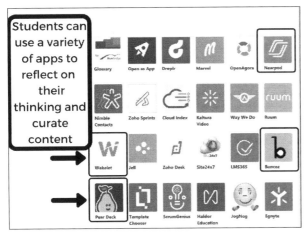

Students can use a variety of apps to reflect on their thinking and curate content

apps within Teams, such as Word, Excel, PowerPoint, or OneNote. Students also can upload documents from their computers, or add connectors with some of students' favorite apps, such as Kahoot, Flipgrid, Wakelet, Buncee, YouTube, and Pear Deck. Teams also allows students to complete assignments, collaborate on projects, create new content, reflect on assignments, and show their creativity through the use of emojis, stickers, gifs, and images, all without leaving Teams.

WHAT'S GREAT IS THAT Microsoft Teams allows students to seamlessly collaborate, have conversations, and streamline workflow. The Class Team automatically comes with the OneNote Class Notebook. With the tabs available in Teams, students can curate external content to support continuous learning. With direct access to resources, assessments, documents, videos, and external websites, students are able to have engaging discussions, create projects, and then reflect on what they have learned through a written reflection, or a video reflection such as Flipgrid, Buncee, or PowerPoint.

GIVES YOU THE INFORMATION by showing you the names of the owners of the Team as well as the names of its members. It also provides the names of team channels or small groups. Microsoft Teams lets students know when new assignments have been created by the teacher along with the due date. Teams lets students know when their assignment has been graded. Teams also lets students know who has posted to the team by time-stamping their response with a date and name. This way teachers can know when the student reflections happened.

IDEAS

- Complete projects from beginning to end within Teams, using Wakelet for research and content curation. Create and present research using PowerPoint, and reflect on the research process using Flipgrid.

- Use Sway to curate the content of a school year in review and reflect on growth using Screencast-O-Matic.

WAKELET

ACCESS FROM ANY DEVICE: wakelet.com

WHAT IS WAKELET? Wakelet is a free visual content curation platform that helps students organize and curate their online information so it is easier to find and share.

GREAT BECAUSE Wakelet allows teachers and students to curate their research and other online learning sources into well-organized silos called collections. Collections can be created collaboratively, and teachers can even create collections to share with students as an additional resource for those students who might need it.

SETUP IS EASY. Sign up at **wakelet.com** by choosing **Sign Up** and then click **New Collection**. For those who wish to simply try it out, there is an option to create a collection without registering.

> Each Wakelet that you create is a social feed in its own right.

> Click **Collections** on your homepage after logging in.

> Click **New Collection**, give your Collection a title, and add a good keyword-based description.

> Newly created collections are set to private by default, so make sure to set your Wakelets to public before sharing with students.

ALLOWS STUDENTS TO curate information from various places and stay organized. Students can save and share videos, articles, images, tweets, links, and much more. The ability to record reflective video directly into Wakelet is now made easy through the integration of Flipgrid's Shorts Camera.

GIVES YOU INFORMATION in one of four display collections: Mood board, Media view, Compact view, and Grid view. Toggle on the "Easy reorder mode" to efficiently move items around.

WHAT IS GREAT IS THAT Wakelet has Microsoft Immersive Reader built in so everything curated is accessible to all. Content can be read aloud and even translated into different languages.

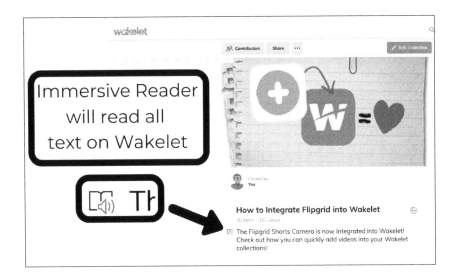

Wakelet also integrates directly into Microsoft Teams and OneNote, allowing students to collaborate on curations. Information also can be saved on the go by using the Wakelet browser extension.

 IDEAS

- Collaborative Research: Students can work together to collect information and collaborate on a topic together.
- Students can create a Wakelet Collection of their work and use the Shorts video feature to explain how this work showcases what they learned during the unit or for the entire year.

SEESAW

ACCESS FROM ANY DEVICE: web.seesaw.me

WHAT IS SEESAW? Seesaw is a digital portfolio app and website that can be a powerful tool for student reflection. We consider Seesaw a making-thinking-visible power tool!

GREAT BECAUSE It provides students with a way to document their learning. They can add both verbal and graphic reflections using videos, photos, and voice recordings. Students can also publish their reflections to your class blog; they may even add a QR code to their reflections, print it, and post it in your class so their peers can scan the code and listen to their recording.

SETUP IS EASY. Create your classes, add your students, then provide them with either a QR code or class code so they can enter your class.

STUDENTS TURN IN WORK BY adding responses and then selecting the green checkmark on the top-right corner of the screen. They can organize their work by using folders if the teacher makes them in advance.

ALLOWS STUDENTS TO

1. Take pictures of their "analog" creations, where they can add drawings, add text, and record their voice to provide insight on their process.

2. Create a video recording within the app.

3. Add a written note.

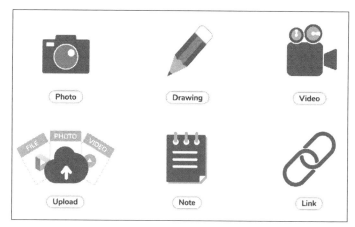

4. Add voice, draw on, or add text to a picture that is already saved on the device, or insert a picture or video that was created in another app or saved on your desktop.

SHOWS YOU INFORMATION THIS WAY on individual feeds, creating a chronological record of their reflections. Using the calendar feature, you can view the work of the entire class or individual students arranged by chronological date.

IDEAS

- **Math**—At the end of a unit or lesson, have students take a picture of an angle and use the drawing tool to identify the type of angle in the photo. Use the record feature to reflect on their learning about angles.

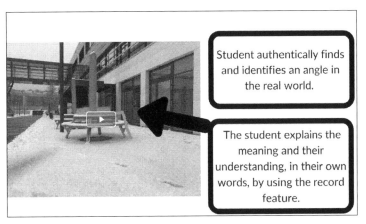

- **Language Arts**—Have students take pictures of their favorite quotes from a book. Use the record feature to have the students explain how this quote was essential in helping them understand the meaning of the book. They can use this thinking strategy and expand on it to write a response to literature when appropriate.

Critical Considerations
WHEN CHOOSING A TOOL

How can you determine the best tools to use with your students? We've collected our guiding principles for you to consider.

Is the app easy to use?

Is it easy for students to set up?

Does it give students a place to leave comments?

Is it always free, or are there costs associated with it?

Can students sign into it with their Microsoft account?

Can students use the tool to share their creations with a global audience?

Can students easily download their creations from it onto their desktop or OneDrive?

Can students use the tool to add text, images, voiceovers, and videos to their work?

Is it available on multiple platforms?

Is the tool FERPA and COPPA compliant?

Does it help students make their thinking visible, give them a voice, and allow them to share their work?

How easily does it allow parents see their children's work?

DIGITAL PORTFOLIOS
Making Student Thinking Visible with Digital Portfolios

> "Become a documentarian of what you do."
>
> —Austin Kleon,
> *Show Your Work*

Making Student Thinking Visible With Digital Portfolios

Digital portfolios provide all of the stakeholders in a student's education with rich information about the student's personal learning and growth. These digital tools give learners a place to make their thinking visible, amplify their voice, and allow them to share their creations for an authentic audience. Portfolios also help students curate their learning artifacts, all the while encouraging them to reflect on and think critically about their learning process.

What's more, when done correctly, digital portfolios should replace the need for traditional methods of assessment and evaluation. With portfolios, stakeholders can gain a more critical perspective into a student's understanding and thinking. Ultimately, this gives us insight into their unique path toward academic growth in a way standardized multiple-choice tests and essays cannot. In short, digital portfolios allow us to understand our students as individual learners; each one is academically strong and proficient in their own way.

Where to Begin
Make parents part of the process.

- Start with parents. Including them in this process will help with both the student's and the portfolio's success.

- Educate parents on the importance of students developing digital literacy skills, digital footprints, and an understanding of their personal web presence. If you need to skip this step, be sure to send home a notice letting parents know that you're putting their children's work online, or else they may not give you the support you need.

- Open a line of communication between home and school around student learning and sharing student work online. Communicate how this promotes an understanding of digital citizenship and online privacy.

- Educate parents on the importance of creating a personal web presence online. After all, we cannot teach digital citizenship in isolation. Students need to be creating content that they are sharing online to fully understand how to use the tools effectively.

THE THREE TYPES OF
Digital Portfolios

PROCESS   SHOWCASE   HYBRID

To make student thinking visible, students use this portfolio to document and reflect on their learning process. The process portfolio is geared toward student reflection on learning and gathering feedback from an outside audience to help improve the learning.

- **The student creates.** This part of the learning process is connected to the students' demonstrations (evidence) of learning (e.g., digital books, video productions, learning journals, and collaborative writing pieces) and can be an assessment for, of, or as learning, because, after all, students are learning while creating this type of portfolio.

- **The student reflects.** As your students work on their demonstration of learning for the portfolio, encourage them to take time and reflect on this process. Help them make their thinking visible by providing guiding questions or a structure for curating these reflective artifacts that they will use for explaining their learning.

- **The student receives feedback.** At this point, the student can share work with classmates or a larger audience to gather ideas or considerations for making the content better before possibly publishing.

- **The student publishes (optional).** As a final step, the student can pick a platform to publish their work. In most cases, publishing is reserved for the showcase pieces we talk about later.

This can be done either with the class, with a tool like Seesaw, or in a more public forum, using a website like Sway.

POSSIBLE TOOLS FOR PROCESS PORTFOLIOS:

- SEESAW
- ADOBE SPARK PAGE
- SWAY
- ONENOTE
- FLIPGRID
- PADLET

Tip for Process Portfolios: As you design your lessons, allot time in your schedule for students to curate comments and screenshots of their work as they go through the process. The artifacts collected should demonstrate evidence of growth.

THE THREE TYPES OF
Digital Portfolios

PROCESS   **SHOWCASE**   **HYBRID**

Showcase portfolios highlight your students' best work. In a showcase portfolio, students publish the work that is most important to them. Because the student chooses the creation that they believe best demonstrates their learning of a specific concept, this portfolio is an assessment of learning.

- **The student creates.** At the end of a unit, students will choose an artifact of learning that best demonstrates growth.

- **The student publishes.** As a final step, the student will now pick a platform to publish their work. This can be done either with the class, with a tool like Seesaw, or in a more public forum, using something like Adobe Page or Sway.

Something to Think About:
Blending Analog and Digital

We've been focusing quite a bit on digital artifacts, but sometimes we don't have everything in a digital format. If your students ever find themselves without a digital copy of a creation they'd like to showcase, they need to look no further than a camera. With a quick tap of their smartphone's camera or a Surface Tablet, they can easily create a digital version of an analog creation, then take that photograph and throw it into Seesaw, Sway, or Adobe Spark Page. The important part here is to capture their thinking about the artifact in the process. This is why Seesaw makes a great platform.

POSSIBLE TOOLS FOR SHOWCASE PORTFOLIOS:

SEESAW

ADOBE SPARK PAGE

SWAY

ONENOTE

FLIPGRID

PADLET

WAKELET

 Tip for Showcase Portfolios: Have students share their work on a social media platform, like Twitter or Instagram, to build an audience and connect with experts who might interact with them to push their thinking and drive their future learning.

THE THREE TYPES OF
Digital Portfolios

PROCESS   SHOWCASE   **HYBRID**

Hybrid portfolios are a combination of process and showcase portfolios. We can use a hybrid portfolio for an assessment of, for, and as learning.

This model allows students to reflect on their learning, choose the pieces they most value and believe best show their growth, and share those pieces with a larger audience.

Note: This portfolio is similar to the process portfolio but adds in a showcase component as well.

- **The student creates.** This part of the learning process is connected to the students' demonstrations of learning (evidence of learning—e.g., digital books, video productions, sketchnotes, and collaborative writing pieces) and is used as an assessment for, of, or as learning.

- **The student reflects.** As your students work on their demonstration of learning for the portfolio, encourage them to take time and reflect on this process. Help them make their thinking visible by providing guiding questions or a structure for curating these reflective artifacts that they will use for explaining their learning.

- **The student receives feedback.** If students would like to receive feedback from a larger audience or even their classmates, the process is simple. Have them digitally capture their work using a camera on a smartphone or a tool like Seesaw. While screencasting, students talk through their learning process, then capture and share the final product on a website or on Seesaw, where they can ask for feedback.

- **The student publishes showcased work.** Students pick one of their favorite process pieces to showcase and share with the world. There can be several process pieces in the portfolio, but they share only the showcase pieces with the world.

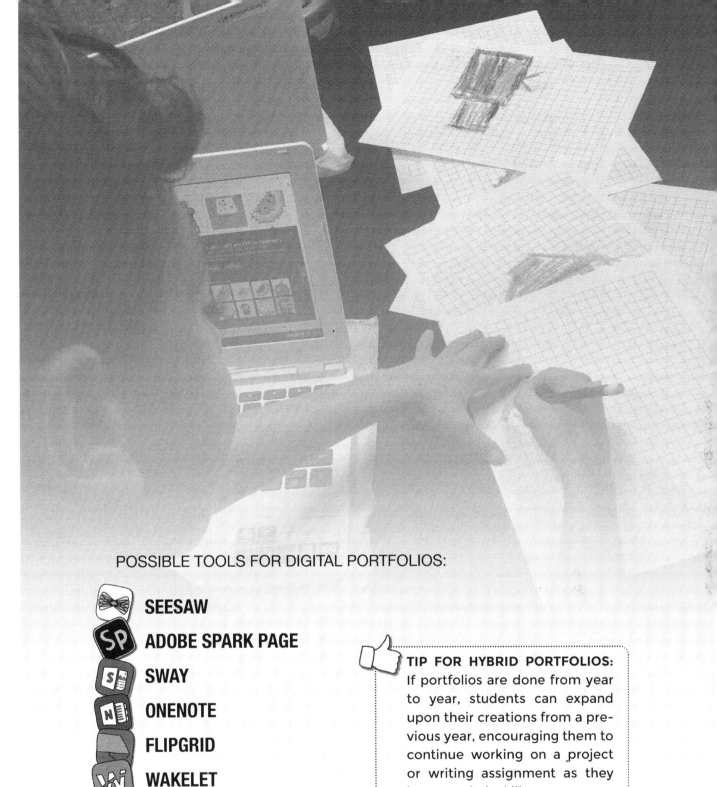

POSSIBLE TOOLS FOR DIGITAL PORTFOLIOS:

- **SEESAW**
- **ADOBE SPARK PAGE**
- **SWAY**
- **ONENOTE**
- **FLIPGRID**
- **WAKELET**

TIP FOR HYBRID PORTFOLIOS:
If portfolios are done from year to year, students can expand upon their creations from a previous year, encouraging them to continue working on a project or writing assignment as they improve their skills.

Highfill, Lisa, Kelly Hilton, and Sarah Landis. 2016. *The HyperDoc Handbook: Digital Lesson Design Using Google Apps*. Irvine, CA: EdTechTeam Press.

McTighe, Jay and Grant Wiggins, " Understanding by Design Framework." ASCD.org, ascd.org/ASCD/pdf/siteASCD/publications/UbD_WhitePaper0312.pdf.

Ritchhart, Ron, Mark Church, and Karin Morrison. 2011. *Making Thinking Visible: How to Promote Engagement, Understanding, and Independence for All Learners*. San Francisco, CA: Jossey-Bass.

Tomlinson, Carol A. 2016. *The Differentiated Classroom: Responding to the Needs of All Learners*. Boston: Published by Pearson Education, Inc., by special arrangement with the Association for Supervision and Curriculum Developement (ASCD).

Tomlinson, Carol A., and Susan D. Allan. 2006. *Leadership for Differentiating Schools & Classrooms*. Heatherton, Vic.: Hawker Brownlow Education.

The Google Infused Classroom

A Guidebook to Making Thinking Visible and Amplifying Student Voice

By Holly Clark and Tanya Avrith

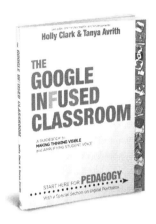

This beautifully designed book offers guidance on using technology to design instruction that allows students to show their thinking, demonstrate their learning, and share their work (and voices!) with authentic audiences. *The Google Infused Classroom* will equip you to empower your students to use technology in meaningful ways that prepare them for the future.

Dive into Inquiry

Amplify Learning and Empower Student Voice

By Trevor MacKenzie

Dive into Inquiry beautifully marries the voice and choice of inquiry with the structure and support required to optimize learning. With *Dive into Inquiry* you'll gain an understanding of how to best support your learners as they shift from a traditional learning model into the inquiry classroom where student agency is fostered and celebrated each and every day.

Inquiry Mindset

Nurturing the Dreams, Wonders, and Curiosities of Our Youngest Learners

By Trevor MacKenzie and Rebecca Bathurst-Hunt

Inquiry Mindset offers a highly accessible journey through inquiry in the younger years. Learn how to empower your students, increase engagement, and accelerate learning by harnessing the power of curiosity. With practical examples and a step-by-step guide to inquiry, Trevor MacKenzie and Rebecca Bathurst-Hunt make inquiry-based learning simple.

Sketchnotes for Educators

100 Inspiring Illustrations for Lifelong Learners

By Sylvia Duckworth

Sylvia Duckworth is a Canadian teacher whose sketchnotes have taken social media by storm. Her drawings provide clarity and provoke dialogue on many topics related to education. This book contains 100 of her most popular sketchnotes with links to the original downloads that can be used in class or shared with colleagues. Interspersed throughout the book are Sylvia's reflections on each drawing and what motivated her to create them, in addition to commentary from other educators who inspired the sketchnotes.

How to Sketchnote

A Step-by-Step Manual for Teachers and Students

By Sylvia Duckworth

Educator and internationally known sketchnoter Sylvia Duckworth makes ideas memorable and shareable with her simple yet powerful drawings. In *How to Sketchnote*, she explains how you can use sketchnoting in the classroom and that you don't have to be an artist to discover the benefits of doodling!

40 Ways to Inject Creativity into Your Classroom with Adobe Spark

By Ben Forta and Monica Burns

Experienced educators Ben Forta and Monica Burns offer step-by-step guidance on how to incorporate this powerful tool into your classroom in ways that are meaningful and relevant. They present 40 fun and practical lesson plans suitable for a variety of ages and subjects as well as 15 graphic organizers to get you started. With the tips, suggestions, and encouragement in this book, you'll find everything you need to inject creativity into your classroom using Adobe Spark.

The HyperDoc Handbook
Digital Lesson Design Using Google Apps

By Lisa Highfill, Kelly Hilton, and Sarah Landis

The HyperDoc Handbook is a practical reference guide for all K–12 educators who want to transform their teaching into blended-learning environments. The HyperDoc Handbook is a bestselling book that strikes the perfect balance between pedagogy and how-to tips while also providing ready-to-use lesson plans to get you started with Hyper-Docs right away.

The InterACTIVE Class
Using Technology to Make Learning More Relevant and Engaging in the Elementary Classroom

By Joe and Kristin Merrill

In this practical and idea-packed book, coauthors, classroom teachers, and edtech experts Joe and Kristin Merrill share their personal framework for creating an interACTIVE classroom. You'll find new ways to inspire young learners to grow and to develop grit as they stretch their thinking and abilities.

ABOUT THE AUTHORS

Holly Clark is an education thought-leader, international speaker, best-selling author, and an advocate for students. She is a twenty-plus year educator who has spent over fifteen years teaching in a 1:1 classroom and over five years as an administrator in both public and private schools. She holds a master's degree in instructional design and educational technology from Columbia University in New York City. Her passion is for helping teachers create classrooms where students want to learn and can become the agents of their own thinking and understanding.

She is a National Board Certified Teacher, Google Certified Innovator, and is now the Chief Learning Officer at The Infused Classroom, Inc. She still spends time co-teaching in classrooms where she helps teachers and schools begin the process of putting students at the center of the learning. Holly consults with schools globally on blended learning environments where meaningful pedagogy is infused with the strategic use of technology. She authors a popular education blog, hollyclark.org, and delivers keynotes to audiences worldwide.

Connect with Holly

Blog: hollyclark.org

Instagram and Twitter @HollyClarkEdu

Email: holly@hollyclark.org

As an advocate for student voice, **Tanya Avrith** believes in the power of storytelling in Education. She has seen stories help kids explore their creativity, construct their identities and connect with others first-hand – a principle that she has the privilege of spreading with the help of Adobe Education, as their Education Evangelist.

Tanya's desire to learn and grow within education technology is insatiable. She completed an MA in EdTech and continued to seek out programs like Apple Distinguished Educator, Google Certified Innovator, and Adobe Education Leader to deepen her knowledge and curiosity. She can often be seen speaking at national and regional EdTech conferences on stage, in a workshop, or the tradeshow floor. Tanya can't stop and won't stop collaborating with teachers and leaders to create more possibilities for students to share their stories.

With a passion for using tools with pedagogical purpose, Tanya co-authored *The Google Infused Classroom*. A book that has helped thousands of teachers worldwide take their edtech education into their own hands – where learning belongs.

Connect with Tanya

Twitter @TanyaAvrith

Website: tanyaavrith.com

Email: tanya@tanyaavrith.com

MEET OUR CONTRIBUTORS

Felisa Ford, a wife, and mother, is a veteran educator with over twenty-four years of classroom and leadership experience. Currently, a digital learning specialist, Felisa provides technology training and support for district staff and students throughout the nation. Felisa has earned many distinctions and certifications in the instructional technology world some of which include Microsoft Innovative Educator Expert, Microsoft Master Trainer, Surface Master Trainer, Buncee Ambassador, Wakelet Ambassador, Flipgrid Certified Educator, Apple Teacher, and many more. Felisa is a proud member of Our Voice Academy. Felisa has presented at many conferences both locally and nationally. Most recently, she presented at FETC as well as NCCE in Seattle, Washington.

Connect with Felisa

Twitter @ApsitFelisa

Joe and Kristin Merrill have a combined nineteen years of teaching experience, where they collaborate to create with one common goal in mind—to create learning experiences for students that are interACTIVE. The Merrills put a new spin on traditional strategies by implementing technology to meet the needs of students.

▶ Connect with Joe & Kristin

Twitter @TheMerrillsEdu

Natasha Rachell, a passionate, veteran educator, is an alternatively certified high school science teacher turned edtech enthusiast! Currently serving as a digital learning specialist, Natasha has immersed herself into the instructional technology space and has earned several distinctions and certifications, some of which include Microsoft Innovative Educator Expert, Google Certified Innovator (MentorMeEdu) and Trainer, Apple Teacher, Surface Master Trainer, and Flipgrid Ambassador. Natasha was selected to take part in the first cohort of Our Voice Academy through EdTechTeam, a group of minority educational technology leaders from across the nation. Natasha has keynoted and presented at many conferences both at the local and national level. She is ecstatic to lead the work as we transition into twenty-first-century classrooms through blended learning opportunities, BYOD, professional learning for instructional technology and digitally connected classrooms.

▶ Connect with Natasha

Twitter @ApsitNatasha

Made in the USA
Columbia, SC
24 May 2020

98305327R00096